CRAZY
TALK

CRAZY

TALK

A Not-So-Stuffy Dictionary of Theological Terms

REVISED AND EXPANDED EDITION

Edited by Rolf A. Jacobson

with

Karl N. Jacobson
Marc D. Olson
Megan J. Thorvilson
Megan L. Torgerson
Hans H. Wiersma

Fortress Press

Minneapolis

First edition published in 2008 by Augsburg Books, an imprint of Augsburg Fortress.

Cover design: Brad Norr
Design and Typesetting: PerfecType, Nashville, TN

Print ISBN: 978-1-5064-1846-9
eBook ISBN: 978-1-5064-1847-6

The paper used in this publication meets the minimum requirements of American National Standard for Information Sciences — Permanence of Paper for Printed Library Materials, ANSI Z329.48-1984.

Manufactured in Canada.

DEDICATION

To:

Ingrid and Gunnar

Hannah, Samuel, and Lucy, Nora, and Claire

Fiona and Freya

Dane and Sigurd

Jacob, Elianna, Marielle, and Garret

CONTENTS

P

R

S

T

INTRODUCTION

Few combinations in life are more gratifying than a good piece of rhubarb pie (no nutmeg) and a cup of strong, black coffee. But one combination that is even more gratifying than this is working with good friends on a project that makes people laugh—and, oh by the way, also teaches them about the love of God. *Crazy Talk* was exactly that kind of project. In *Crazy Talk*, we tried to make theology funny and joyful.

Not everyone in the Christian tradition enjoys a good joke or even a good laugh. *The Rule of Saint Benedict* for example, which is one of the most important documents in Western Civilization, scolds, "Be not ready and quick to laugh, for it is written, 'The fool lifts up his voice in laughter' (Eccles. 21:23)." It is called the "rule" of Benedict, after all. And we never have liked church rules too much. They can be sort of a buzz kill or a killjoy. And one should never kill joy.

After all, our Lord and Savior Jesus Christ said, "There is joy in the presence of the angels of God" (see Luke 15:10). That's right. There is joy! Theological talk—our earthly conversation about the things of God—ought to reflect the language of heaven. It ought to be joyful.

But theological talk also needs to be faithful. So in creating the jokes, we also strived to be faithful to what the Bible and the Christian tradition have said about God. After all, the Lord and Savior also said, "Every scribe who has been trained for the kingdom of heaven is like the master of a household who brings out of his treasure what is new and what is old" (Mark 13:52). Meaning, we think, "Don't let the jokes get in the way of the Truth." We hope we haven't.

Over the years, we have received generous and kind feedback. One mother told me that as she was driving on the freeway way to a church gathering, her high-school–aged son was reading articles from *Crazy Talk*. "We got to laughing so hard that suddenly we realized we had driven an hour past our exit." Think of the waste of gas! So climate change is our fault, too. More's the pity.

We hope you enjoy this new edition of *Crazy Talk* so that you find joy on your journey. But don't miss the exit.

Rolf Jacobson

absence of God \ab-suhnts-uhv-GAHD\ n. + prep. + n.

"Please excuse the Almighty's absenteeism, God had the stomach flu." Signed, Epstein's mother.

Have you ever noticed that there's never a cop around when you need one? Or a taxi? Or a BLT? It sometimes feels that way with God too. Where is God when you need God? Where, for that matter, is God when you *don't* need God? But have you looked everywhere? Like, even in the downstairs bathroom?

Actually, God is hiding, but just from you, probably because of something you did. Just kidding.

It can be hard for us when it feels like God is nowhere to be found, especially when we are struggling. But we have good news for you.

3

The Gospel of John says, "No one has ever seen God. It is God the only Son, who is close to the Father's heart, who has made him known" (John 1:18). This means that we can always find God in Jesus.

And here's a little more good news—and some good advice as well—this time from the first letter of John: "No one has ever seen God; but if we love one another, God lives in us, and his love is perfected in us" (1 John 4:12). We can bring God's presence to life for people who are hurting, scared, or suffering by showing up and reflecting the love of God in a supportive act or comforting word.

See also: Christ (Messiah); immanence of God; incarnation; omnipresence; presence of God; theodicy

absolution \ab-suh-ʟoo-shun\ n.

A series of words that, when spoken to a repentant sinner, result in that sinner's complete forgiveness—much to the chagrin of the self-righteous.

The absolution isn't really a solution at all, at least not in the liquid sense. Rather, the absolution is an announcement.

When the words of absolution are announced, forgiveness happens. The absolution is what linguists like to call "performative language." That's a highfalutin' way to say that the absolution *does what it says*—like when you say, "I bet you five dollars," the words do what they say.

Jesus is all about setting sinners free (see John 8:31–35). But how will sinners know they're forgiven if no one tells them? So words are needed. And not just any words, but words that announce forgiveness is given. That way, the words accomplish what they are designed to accomplish, namely, the forgiveness of sins. To be more precise, the sinner *experiences* forgiveness.

Because where there is forgiveness, there is also life and salvation and cash prizes (okay, maybe no cash).

So here are the words: "In Jesus' name, I announce to you the forgiveness of all your sins."

What's that? You don't think you have the power to forgive sins? Check out what Jesus said: "If you forgive the sins of any, they are forgiven" (John 20:23). He promised. You say it. Said. Done.

See also: forgiveness; means of grace; promise; repentance

adiaphora \ah-dee-AH-fuh-ruh\ n.

Churchy stuff that doesn't really matter—so, therefore, to certain stuffy types of churchy people, this stuff matters way too much.

In Greek, an *adiaphoron* is an "indifferent thing"—something of so little consequence that it's not worth fighting about. Curiously, over the centuries, Christians have found all kinds of *adiaphora* to fight

A

about. Granted, there are some "necessary things"—some essentials—worth an argument. "That Christ died for our sins . . . was buried . . . and raised on the third day"—these are things of "first importance," according to the apostle Paul.

But what about unnecessary things (i.e., *adiaphora*)? Back in Paul's day there was a question about food sacrificed to idols. Corinth was a city filled with shrines to various Greek gods. Some Christians thought that food that had been sacrificed to those gods should not be eaten. Others didn't think it was that big a deal. The Apostle Paul told those Corinthians, *Go ahead, eat food used in idol worship!* But he also said, *Be careful! Your freedom with food might not go over so well with those who are weak in faith* (see 1 Corinthians 8:1–13). In other words, Paul said, When deciding how to behave regarding something that isn't a big deal, consider what your neighbor will think about it. Use the idea of "love your neighbor" as your guide.

During the time of the Reformation, there were some nasty scraps about what was and was not *adiaphora*. Around the year 1530, certain unstuffy church types asserted that Christians do not have to agree on every God-blessed detail of the Christian life. In other words, not all worship services have to have the same style, music, dress codes, seating arrangements, and so on. Later, these unstuffy types said, in effect, *If it's not forbidden in Scripture, go ahead and do it*; *unless someone says, "You have to do this to be a Christian,"* then don't *do it*. In other words, do what you want in matters that are no big deal. If someone says you have to do it to be a real Christian, then don't. And yet later, a pastor named Rupert Meldenius wrote, "In essentials, unity; in nonessentials, liberty; and in all things, love."

(Actually, he wrote, *In necessariis unitas, in dubiis libertas, in omnibus caritas*. If your name was Rupert, you'd talk like that, too.)

The problem with *adiaphora* is that what's unnecessary and non-essential to one person may be necessary and essential to another. Take for example the wearing of robes by pastors and others who lead worship. There's no commandment that goes, "Thou shalt not wear special garments during worship." (Although we would hope, for the sake of decency, that all worship leaders at least wear *something* during worship.) The tradition of wearing robes in worship goes back to the worship of ancient Israel. Furthermore, worship leaders getting all gussied up has been a part of Christian worship for many centuries. Still, since there's no divine commandment for or against it, it shouldn't matter if your pastor wears a robe or not. On the face of it, then, wearing a robe in worship is an unnecessary thing: an *adiaphoron*.

Here's where it can get complicated. What if *you're* the pastor, and you prefer not to wear robes. And what if there's a church meeting where you're told that you must wear robes in church. What do you do? Do you put up a fight because an *adiaphoron* is being turned into a necessary thing (and lose your job in the process)? Or do you figure, *Well, since it really doesn't matter to me either way, and since it matters so much to you, I'll wear the stinkin' robe, okay? Everybody happy now?*

That's *adiaphora* for ya.

See also: bishop, pastor/priest, Reformation, tradition, worship

adoptionism \uh-DAHP-shun-ih-zuhm\ n.

The heretical teaching that Jesus didn't become God's Son until, like, age thirty.

In the second century CE, some Christian groups weren't impressed by the story of Mary and baby Jesus and the whole virgin birth thing. They preferred Mark's Gospel (with its lack of a birth

account) and interpreted the story of Jesus' baptism (see Mark 1:9–11) as the moment when God *adopted* Jesus as the divine Son. Adoptionism was one of the earliest Christian heresies. Like almost all of the earliest alternative viewpoints of Jesus, Adoptionism "can't handle the truth" that the immortal, infinite, omnipotent God could be

fully present in a mortal, finite, impotent (not to mention runny-nosed) baby. As if waiting until age thirty fixed this logical objection!

See also: Christology; heresy; hypostatic union; incarnation

agnosticism \ag-NAH-stih-sih-zuhm\ n.

The intellectual stance of doubting everything except one's own opinion.

Descartes said, "I think, therefore I am." The agnostic says, "I think, and that is all I know." Agnosticism—which means "without knowledge"—describes a school of thought that teaches, "I don't know. *You* don't know. *No one can* know." This position is the intellectual equivalent of a "Do Not Disturb" sign. Some contend that it's the only rational position when it comes to matters of faith. Agnostics generally discount some key aspects of Christianity: revelation, faith, belief, the Holy Spirit . . . and having a sense of humor.

See also: atheism; experience; faith; Holy Spirit; revelation

angel \ān-juhl\ n.

Divine beings, heavenly servants of God, known as purveyors of some godly message, such as recipes for light and delicious food cakes and impossibly fine pastas, or the somewhat rougher traditions of motorcycle fellowship.

Neither fish nor fowl, an angel is a messenger who bears a tiding from God. In art angels are most often depicted with wings upon the back—sometimes two, sometimes six—but it should be noted that in the Bible, angels most often do not have wings and seem to appear much like people. There is one biblical passage that describes a type of angel that has six wings—Isaiah 6. If you're wondering whether the six-winged angel flies faster than the other varieties, the answer is no—two wings are used for flying, two cover the eyes, and two cover the feet (Isaiah 6:2). (Now, whether a laden or un-laden angel makes better time remains a separate matter.)

The angel has long been one of the most compelling biblical creatures, inspiring artwork throughout the centuries, lines of collectable figurines, and the occasional melodrama. Despite the fascination,

A

or perhaps because of it, there are many misconceptions about angels. The angel is not primarily one's "wingman," some sort of divine insurance policy, or an airborne-side-winding-muscle-for-hire (although the Bible does attest to God sending angels to watch over God's chosen people or person; see Genesis 24:7, 20; Psalm 91:11). Neither is an angel the next stage in human evolution, what good little boys and girls morph into when they die. Every time you hear a bell ring it means . . . it's lunch-time, or break's over, or Pavlov's messing with his dog again—*not* that an angel gets his wings. Angels are creatures made by God, much like human beings, only of a slightly different order. Maybe an equation would be helpful at this point: as chimpanzees are to people, so people are to angels—as far as the human creature is above the lovable chimp, so are angels that much higher than humans.

First and foremost, angels are messengers, beings who have been entrusted with the task of delivering God's Word. With their winged harking (or is it harping?), angels herald important events, give instruction, or issue warning. The messages angels deliver vary: Hagar is promised well-being for her son; Abraham and Sarah are promised a son; Joseph is convinced to stick with Mary; and of course Jesus' birth and resurrection are declared first by angels. In short, angels communicate God's will to their fellow creatures, and in this regard Shakespeare is right when he says human beings are like angels (*Hamlet* 2.2), for this is the point at which normal, everyday dopes like us are at our most angelic—when we share the message of Jesus with our fellow creatures.

See also: gospel; Word of God

anger of God \Ān-guhr-uhv-GAHD\ n. + prep. + n.

The puzzling concept that God loves our neighbors so much that God gets angry at us when we do (or don't do) things that cause them to suffer.

People like a nice God—one who is tame, like a kitty, all cute and cuddly and loving. People like a God of love. As the character Ricky Bobby says in *Talladega Nights*, "I like the Christmas Jesus best . . . I like the baby version the best." In fact, people like this "nice" God so much that they tend to find the whole idea of the "anger of God' off-putting and downright medieval.

Sometimes people even say stupid things like this: "The New Testament God is a God of love, but the Old Testament God is a God of anger." To repeat: this is stupid.

Key point number one: God's love is connected to God's anger. Without the "anger of God," the very idea of the "love of God" is just as silly and sentimental as, well, a stuffed toy lion. It is because God loves us people—all of us people—that he gets mad. Think of it like this:

A. God loves you just the way you are.
B. God loves your neighbor just the way he or she is.
C. God gets angry at you when you cause your neighbor to suffer. Why? Because God is petty, vindictive, narrow-minded, and medieval? *No!* Because God loves your neighbor and hates to see your neighbor suffer! (See B.)

A

D. God gets angry at your neighbor when he or she causes you to suffer. Why? Because God is a sadistic control freak who loves to punish people? *No!* Because God loves you and hates to see you suffer.

Key point number two: God's anger is temporary. Psalm 30:5 says, "God's anger is but for a moment, his favor is for a lifetime." God gets angry when there is something to be angry about. When that something-to-be-angry-about goes away, God's anger goes away. Oh, sure, it is true that with more than 7.5 billion people on the earth, there is probably enough evil going on that God is always angry at somebody. But God is not always angry with everybody. Lincoln would have said, "God is angry with all of the people some of the time, God is angry with some of the people all of the time, but God is not angry with all of the people all of the time."

Key point number three: God's love is permanent. God continues to love us even when he is angry at us. And God's love will never change. God loves us so much that he sent Jesus to us, and in our place, Jesus accepted the consequences of our sins. Because of Jesus, no matter how angry God might get at the evil we do, we don't have to pay the consequences for our sins.

See also: atonement; attributes of God; love

anthropology \an-thruh-PAH-luh-jee\ n.

The central teachings about the nature of human beings, the most important elements of which are, naturally, not about human beings but about God.

Theology is crazy talk, and you've probably already figured out why. Check it out. According to some teachers, the most important concept in the study of theology is anthropology. Let us translate that into plain English: when studying the things of God, the most important concepts are the teachings about the nature of human beings.

Picture that duck on TV who sells insurance shaking his head in confusion.

Wait, there's more. According to some teachers, the most important thing about anthropology is the relation of humans to God.

Picture the duck having an aneurism.

The point is that square one in theology has to do with the basic nature of the relationship between God and humanity. If you get these wrong, well, you're pretty much out of luck. But if you get these right, *glory hallelujah!*

We can focus on two central points. First, human beings are created in the image of God. See Genesis 1:26. The basic idea is that when God created humanity, God endowed us with something special that no other creature was given. Second, the human condition is fallen, sinful, and broken. The basic idea is that we need rescuing from our very nature, from our very selves.

This is who you are. And once you know that, you're off to a great start in theology.

See also: creation; fall, the; grace; image of God; sin

antichrist \AN-tee-krīst\ n.

The president, the pope, and/or your mother-in-law all rolled into one. If and when The Big Antichrist actually appears, it will probably look more like your grandma.

The antichrist is generally viewed by some Christians as some kind of huge, powerful international person or thing that controls all the world and faces off with the good Christians in the final struggle between good and evil.

Unfortunately, that's also generally wrong. The idea of "the antichrist" is pieced together from lots of different biblical references. And then people go and make a huge deal of something that the Bible itself doesn't even make a big deal about.

If we asked you where the antichrist appeared in the Bible, you'd probably say in Revelation . . . and you'd be totally wrong. The word *antichrist* only appears in the books of 1 and 2 John. Don't believe us? Read it and weep: 1 John 2:18–22; 4:3; 2 John 1:7.

A

First John 2:18 suggests that there is more than just one antichrist: "As you have heard that antichrist is coming, so now many antichrists have come." And check this out: "Who is the liar but the one who denies that Jesus is the Christ? This is the antichrist" (1 John 2:22). This means that the antichrist could pretty much be any of us—including your grandma.

The reason you probably got to thinking the antichrist was in Revelation is because that's what everyone seems to think. The line of thought goes like this: Revelation is about the end of the world, the antichrist comes at the end of the world, ergo we can do some fancy addition and figure that the "dragon" or "beast" of Revelation is the same as the antichrist of 1 John. But in this case, 2 + 2 = 5, which you just know is wrong.

Have you heard of the beast? Well, the beast is a figure in Revelation who is all mean and kills believers and stuff. (Read Revelation 13 to hear all about it. It's good stuff.) So technically, that character is indeed an antichrist—but it is not *the* antichrist. It just makes a better movie script if there's one big, bad villain who's easy to tell from the good guy.

Throughout history, lots of folks have been labeled the antichrist. It's basically the ultimate smear tactic. If someone can peg their least-favorite politician as the antichrist, then people can point and scream, "Evil!" Never mind that Revelation clearly depicts the beast as sleek, suave, and stylish—more like James Bond than Jack the Ripper—and that just makes him harder to find.

In the end, don't focus on the antichrist, who is *against Christ*, but on Christ, who is *for us*. And don't be scared by the image of some drag-nasty, horror-show monster. After all, Christ is more powerful than any beast, real or imagined. As the good book says, "If God is for us, who is against us?" (Romans 8:31).

See also: apocalypse; apocalyptic literature; rapture

antinomian \an-tih-NOH-mee-uhn\ adj.

antinomianism \an-tih-NOH-mee-uhn-ih-zuhm\ n.

The belief—mistakenly held by some Christians—that the rules don't apply; the mistaken notion that since God loves us, God must not expect us to keep his law.

Antinomians believe the law serves no purpose for the followers of Jesus. Even better, antinomians have theological backing! Antinomian reasoning goes like this: since God saves us by grace through faith *apart from the works of the law*, therefore, once we are saved, we don't need the law.

A religion without rules! Where do we sign up?!

There's something almost right about this way of thinking. Antinomians, you see, are confident that Jesus transforms people not with law but with love. Antinomians know that the Holy Spirit inspires believers to things like love, joy, peace, patience, kindness, generosity, faithfulness, gentleness, and self-control. You can't legislate such virtues, and there's no law against them (as the apostle Paul points out in Galatians 5:22–23). So, this line of thinking goes, just preach grace and the forgiveness of sins, and these things will take care of themselves.

The problem, of course, is that Christians remain sinful even after they are saved, and thus they always need the law to help keep the effects of sin in check. Think of it this way: no, you don't need the law to be saved, but your neighbor still needs you to keep the law so that your neighbor's life will be better.

See also: justification; law; sanctification; simultaneously saint and sinner

apocalypse \uh-pah-kuh-lihps\ n.

The fact that, when it comes to the future of the planet, we human beings are insecure and fascinated at the same time; also one of Hollywood's favorite subjects.

apocalyptic literature \uh-pah-kuh-lihp-tihk-LIH-tuhr-uh-chuhr\ n.

Writings that envision the end of the world as we know it—and what comes after.

Hollywood has made billions selling us tickets to the apocalypse, whether it comes via alien invasion (*War of the Worlds*, *Men in Black*), nuclear war (*Dr. Strangelove*), global warming (*The Day after Tomorrow*), deadly disease (*12 Monkeys*, *Contagion*), evolved machines (*The Matrix*), evolved monkeys (*Planet of the Apes*), big rocks (*Armageddon*), big lizards (*Godzilla*), or big "lasers" (*Austin Powers: International Man of Mystery*). Then there are all those films about what life might be like *after* the apocalypse (*Mad Max*, *Zombieland*, *Book of Eli*). We loves us some doomsday—as long as we can munch popcorn and watch it on the big screen!

If they made the Bible's concluding apocalypse, the book of Revelation, into a movie, it would dwarf all the others in terms of scale and budget. Especially if they cast Clint Eastwood as one of the four horsemen (which they've done once already), Amy Schumer as the lead angel, Bill Murray as the beast ("dogs and cats living together!"), and RuPaul, who would bring a certain campiness to the great whore of Babylon part.

In Greek, the word *apocalypse* comes from a word that means "to uncover, to unveil, to reveal." There are other examples of apocalyptic literature throughout the Bible, for example, in the book of Daniel and Mark 13. But the bulk of it is there at the end of the book of the Apocalypse (aka Revelation). Because the book contains visions of a new earth, the word *apocalypse* came to be associated with the total destruction of the present earth (with the possible exception of cockroaches). But the original function of the book was to comfort and reassure groups of Christians who were (and are) experiencing persecution and hardship. Out of the strange, vivid, and often violent imagery of the Bible's apocalypse comes a hopeful message: God is with you in in times of trial and tribulation; the brutal tyrants of this age will not have the last word; the Word of God endures forever; a new world is in the making; hugs all around.

See also: atonement; justice; redemption; revelation; two kingdoms

apocrypha \uh-PAH-krih-fuh\ n.

A part of your Bible that isn't in your friend's Bible; a part of your friend's Bible that isn't in your Bible; the middle section of your Bible that isn't included in "The Bible."

Confused? Bear with us while we offer a little mind-numbing background. The thirty-nine books of Old Testament were written in Hebrew. Those books were translated into Greek once Greek became the daily language of the Jewish people. Some additional Jewish writings were composed in Greek. Just to confuse matters,

A

some books were written in Hebrew, translated into Greek, but the original Hebrew copies were lost.

Asleep yet? So the question is, what books are officially considered "in" the Old Testament?

Different Christian groups answer the question differently. Protestant groups followed the lead of the Jewish faith and accept only the thirty-nine books for which Hebrew copies still exist. The Roman Catholic Church accepts an additional seven books or parts of books: Tobit; Judith; Wisdom of Solomon; 1 and 2 Macabees; Sirach; Baruch; and some additions to Esther, Daniel, and Jeremiah. Various Orthodox churches accept all of these books plus some more: Prayer of Manasseh; Psalm 151; 1, 2 and 3 Esdras; and 3 and 4 Maccabees.

In a coma yet? Many study Bibles print the apocryphal books in a separate section between the Old and New Testaments. Just to make things easy, all Christian groups agree that the New Testament has only twenty-seven books. Thank God—we don't think you could survive a longer essay.

See also: Bible; canon; Catholic; Orthodox Church

apologetics \uh-pah-luh-JEH-tihks\ n.

An explanation of the reason for the hope that is in you (1 Peter 3:15)—in case anyone should ask.

Gee, you don't have to get all defensive . . . except when you do—like when you have to explain why you believe in God and what you believe. This is called "apologetics." (Originally, an *apologia* was a "reasoned defense," not a mealy-mouthed *mea culpa*.) That is, there may come a time when you have to explain to people why you believe, for instance, that God exists, that Jesus is God in human form, that God-in-human-form was crucified like a common criminal, that Christ was raised from the dead, and that because of it all, your sins are forgiven and you, too, will one day live with Christ for all eternity.

See also: theology; witness

apostasy \uh-PAH-stuh-see\ n.

The reverse of repentance; coming to one's senses or changing one's mind about belief in the unbelievable.

Apostasy sounds like a stance against all things Stacy (*apo* = "against" + *Stacy* = if you knew her, you'd understand what we mean, but this has nothing to do with her). But the term means the deliberate abandonment of previous loyalties or beliefs. In the Bible it is usually associated with sin, transgression, idolatry, and other grievous sins. Apostasy, like slouching, is usually obvious (Jeremiah 2:19) and can be overcome (Ezekiel 37:23) through repentance . . . or re-repentance or re-re-repentance.

Note: It takes a disciple to apostatize, but then the apostatized can be returned to disciplehood by the grace of God (again see Ezekiel 37:23). The point is that we all have a bit of both in us all the time.

See also: blasphemy; fall, the; heresy; repentance; simultaneously saint and sinner; sin

apostle \uh-PAH-suhl\ n.

A person who is sent to bring such good news that he or she must be stoned.

apostolic \a-puh-STAH-lihk\ adj.

The condition of having been sent to bring good news and of not-yet-being-stoned.

From the Greek word meaning "sent out" (as in "a postal worker"), apostles are women and men who are *sent out* by God—often wearing smart caps and striped shorts and carrying mailbags chock full of personal letters from God for everyone in the world. They are often accused of being drunk (see Acts 2:15), but that's just the Holy

Spirit shining through. For prime examples of stoned apostles and their apostolic monologues, check out the first few chapters of the book of Acts.

Originally, the term referred to Jesus' first followers sent out to preach the good news, people such as the original twelve disciples. But not Judas Iscariot, who was held out of training camp because he wanted thirty silver pieces more in salary. But yes, that does include Matthias, who was promoted from the minor leagues to replace Judas (see Acts 1:12–14), and also Paul, who originally played for the other team but was signed as a free agent after an encounter with the team owner (see Acts 9). It also includes all the other men—and women, like Junia (see Romans 16:7)!—to whom Jesus appeared in the flesh and whom Jesus sent out to bring the good news to the rest of the world. And don't forget Mary Magdalene—"the apostle to the apostles"—the first person sent out to announce that Christ had risen!

Primed by the blowout party at Pentecost, the apostles were sent off with the message of Jesus' death and resurrection and the news that the entire world was reconciled to God through Jesus. Early Christian tradition held that each of the first apostles founded churches in various corners of the world—all the way from Ethiopia to India, China, and beyond. Legends and stories also exist about the gruesome ends that most met at the hands of unreceptive audiences and offended religious and government officials.

If prophets were the forerunners of Jesus the Messiah, the apostles were the follow-up folks. They were sent to announce Christ's resurrection, preach, teach, baptize, and minister in God's name. The original apostles laid out the reality of both sin and forgiveness in a direct and personal way. This kind of law-and-gospel thing met resistance, fear, and anger from many in the various audiences they encountered but also a fair amount of belief.

Once the original apostles died, there were no replacements. But the idea of the church being *apostolic* remains important. The church is apostolic in two ways. First, we preach the same message—the same good news—the first apostles did. Second, our mission is the same as theirs—God continues to send us out to announce to the world "that Christ died for our sins" (1 Corinthians 15:3).

See also: church; disciple; evangelical; martyr; saint

ascension \uh-SEHN-shun\ n.

More of a lateral move than an outright promotion for Jesus.

The Bible reports the physical flight of Jesus—from earth to heaven—occurred after his resurrection and before Pentecost. This doctrine raises some questions about stuff like heaven, the current location of God, and the use of helium among the Christians of the first century. Practically, the absence of the risen Jesus placed the responsibility for the ongoing ministry of proclamation on the apostles, but the Holy Spirit was sent to fire up their ministry. Theologically, the ascension means that Jesus is at God's "right hand"—fully equal with God—and that he is present throughout creation and active in the ongoing reconciliation of the universe.

See also: apostle; glory; heaven; Pentecost; resurrection; Trinity

atheism \Ā-thee-ih-zuhm\ n.

The belief that you are solely at the whim of natural powers—mostly likely because you can't handle living soulfully at the whim of God's power.

When we get mad at God—unlike when we get mad at our parents or the television remote control—we can decide that God doesn't exist. To claim atheism, you likely believe that the very idea of God is too silly for a person of any intelligence. No higher power reigns or ever reigned. Instead, humanity decides its own fate and can sleep in on Sunday morning.

The problem is, as the saying goes, that if you don't believe in something, you'll fall for anything. Humans place their trust in things they deem powerful, no matter how hard they fight for their perceived independence. A person who claims not to believe in God likely puts something else in God's place, like money, prestige, power, youthful good looks, or fat-free half-and-half. All of which fall apart. In other words, no one can truly be an atheist since everyone puts their faith in things they deem to be more powerful than they are.

Ironically, the stance of not believing in God does not make God cease to exist. God is not the power of positive thinking that needs to be believed in order to exist. God is—whether you like it or not. God continues to work in your life even when you deny it. If you're going to put your faith in something anyway, you might as well put it in Someone who cares, forgives, and loves.

See also: agnosticism; free will

atonement \uh-TOHN-muhnt\ n.

Sort of like attunement—the act by which the person next to you quits singing off pitch and gets in sync with the choir— atonement is the act of God by which God takes us, who are out of sync with both God and neighbor, and sets us right.

Funny thing—back in the day, Christian leaders would get together now and then to settle up issues of church teaching. These Christian conventions (councils) started with the Council of Nicea in 325 CE. The conventions continued for many centuries after that. During these conventions, many questions were settled—big questions like, Who is Jesus? (answer: God *and* human); who is the Holy Spirit? (answer: God); and who is Mary? (answer: the mother of God). Small questions were settled too, like, Should you castrate yourself? (answer: no); and should you re-baptize former heretics? (answer: only some). How many bishops does it take to make another bishop? (answer: three, but they don't fit in a light bulb). Yet, amazingly, not one single council addressed the question of atonement, that is, of how Jesus' death and resurrection save us. Why didn't they address this? We guess they weren't arguing about it, or at least there were no big squabbles.

Maybe you've heard *atonement* defined as "at-one-ment"; that is, through Christ's death and resurrection, we are made "at one" with God. That's a good image. In John 17 Jesus prays, "The glory that you have given me I have given them, so that they may be one, as we are one, I in them and you in me, that they may become completely one." In Romans 6 Paul says that baptism joins us together with Christ, making us one with his death and resurrection. In Galatians

26

3 we are told that in baptism, all human differences disappear, "for all of you are one in Christ Jesus." That's a lot of at-one-ment to be sure.

As to the question of *how* Jesus does this, theologians have found three main metaphors in the New Testament.

1. Jesus as money. A first metaphor is *ransom*. You may have thought to yourself, *Jesus is so money.* And you are right. Jesus declares that he "came not to be served but to serve, and to give his life as a ransom for many." The image here is that God paid Satan a ransom—Jesus—making satisfaction for our sins and setting us free. But some people didn't find the "ransom" idea of atonement very satisfying (no pun intended). Why would God owe anything to that old devil? A guy named Anselm preferred a second metaphor.

2. Jesus as Hermione Granger. This metaphor is *obedience*. If you've read your Harry Potter, you know that Hermione is the most obedient student ever—she never skips class, forgets to do her homework, or breaks a rule. Anselm insisted that it's not about what God owes the devil (which is nothing) but what we owe God: complete obedience. God wanted to unite with us but couldn't because of our disobedience. So God went all Hermione Granger and took human form in the person of Jesus, who was "obedient unto death—even death on a cross" (Philippians 2:8).

3. Jesus as the Terminator. The metaphor here is "victory in battle." The battle is between God (the good guy) and death, suffering, and the devil (the bad guys). A guy named Athanasius saw death, sickness, suffering, and evil as the real problem. Through Jesus' death and resurrection—"I'll be back"—God opens a can of kickbutt on sin, death, and the devil. As Paul writes, "The sting of death is sin. . . . But thanks be to God, who gives us victory through our Lord Jesus Christ" (1 Corinthians 15:56–57).

In the end, perhaps it's best to say that it matters not so much *how* Christ's cross does what it does but rather *that* Christ's cross does what it does for you.

See also: happy exchange; heresy; Jesus; justification; sacrifice; simultaneously saint and sinner

attributes of God \A-trih-byoots-uhv-GAHD\ n.

The qualifications we look for in a spouse but secretly think describe ourselves.

The personal ads in *Spirituality Search Illustrated* (if such a magazine existed) include listings for "human beings in search of a god." Like this one: *Unrighteous, sinful, mortal, finite, suffering, faulty, changing, unfaithful, partially knowing human being looking for stable, long-distance relationship, for this lifetime or longer, with compatible deity. Deity must be righteous, holy, immortal, impassible, perfect, immutable, faithful, omniscient, able-to-be-incarnate, gracious, merciful, slow to anger, abiding in steadfast love, and suitably godlike to inspire worship. No wrathful, vengeful, or spiteful deities need apply. No pets. No smokers.*

Whether or not you're currently on the prowl for your next object of worship, once you ask the question, "What's God like?," you're talking about the attributes of God. The Bible is the source from which lists of God's attributes are built, and there are at least two ways most people go about the task of listing God's attributes.

A

First, there's what we like to call the *via negativa* (Latin crazy talk for "the negative way"). This is also called *apophatic* theology. Negative theologians prefer to list all of the things God (or divinity) is *not*. Mostly, this is done in a negative comparison to some of the more undesirable attributes of humanity, because, as negative theologians are irritatingly eager to point out, God is *not like* people. People are mortal, so God is immortal. People are finite, so God is infinite. People are passible (which means we suffer), so God is impassible. Here is a biblical example: "God is not a human being, that he should lie" (Numbers 23:19). The *via negativa* can be pretty satisfying. Think of how much fun a toddler has screaming the word "No!"

Second, there's the *via positiva*, also known as *kataphatic* theology. Don't be mistaken by the word *positive*. These folks aren't all sunshine and roses. This just means they'll go ahead and take a stab at saying what God *is* or is like. Like the Negative Nellies, the Positivies Pollies tend to start with qualities and attributes of humans— they just start with the good ones. It's a simple formula: just take something you like (say, "goodness," for example), put it on steroids (or Divine Growth Hormone, for which there is no test), and attach it to God. People are powerful, so God is all-powerful (in *Crazy Talk* we call this *omnipotent*; see OMNIPOTENCE). People know stuff, so God knows all the stuff (*Crazy Talk* = *omniscient*; see OMNISCIENCE). People are present, so God is everywhere present (*Crazy Talk* = *omnipresent*; see OMNIPRESENCE). A biblical example: "God is merciful and gracious, slow to anger, and abounding in steadfast love and faithfulness" (Exodus 34:6).

Two words of warning. First, the impulse to start with yourself—what you like or don't like, what you want or don't want—is dangerous. You might end up worshiping a big and distorted picture of yourself. That's why the final test for any list of attributes is the Bible, and more precisely, Jesus. Second, you can't have a relationship with a list of attributes. You worship and love God, not some list.

See also: idol; omnipotence; omnipresence; omniscience; ontology; theology

baptism \BAP-tih-zuhm\ n.

The cosmic dunk tank (or if you're scared, the spiritual sprinkler); the big bath; a dip in the deep end of the sacred pool; the only rinsing your soul will ever need.

Baptism is viewed by many as a one-time event of such meaning and incomparable effect that, once endured, it is easily forgotten or ignored. Baptism is viewed by many others as an event of such lasting, life-altering, Holy-Spirit powered impact that one has to do it over and over and over again.

Baptism is often thought of as an initiation, an event that ushers one into community. It is ironic, then, that this unifying event is so often the cause of conflict, argument, and discord. It is one of the central practices of the Christian church, and incredible variety exists

31

regarding how it is done, upon whom it is visited, and by whom it is performed. How it is done: by sprinkling, by pouring, or by straight-up, full-on dunking—every practice may be observed. On whom it is visited: from the drooling infant gumming her binky to the drool-

ing adult gumming his Jell-O—baptism is valid at any age. Who performs it: although normally performed by a pastor, technically just about anyone may perform a baptism, including Sally Q. Pew-sitter or some guy off the street. People fight over these things, but we've given you the truth. If you decide to quit reading right now, well, we certainly wouldn't blame you, but we would have to call you a quitter, and you wouldn't want to live with that, would you?

But don't lose hope. Just remember that a lot of what people argue about is the little stuff. Remember that the Bible does not actually give us clear instructions about the details of baptism. (That is why folks fight about them.) Rather, the Bible stresses what God does in baptism—this is the key. A good place to start is the story of Jesus' boy Philip and the Ethiopian dude (Acts 8:26–39). Read it. Go ahead, take a minute—we'll wait.

So what makes a baptism? (1) God's Word: the E-dude is reading Isaiah (53:7–8, specifically), and Philip tells him Jesus' story (a little something we like to call the *good news*); and (2) water: E-dude says, "Look, here is water!" And that's it. God's Word + water =

baptism. Notice, too, that our boy the E-dude doesn't really do anything, and neither does Philip. Baptism is about what God does, not what the baptizer or baptizee does. What's really cool about this is that baptism is connected to the death and resurrection of Jesus—to what God is doing in the death and new life of Christ. In baptism God joins us to Christ's death and resurrection (see Romans 6:3). This is important because it shows what happens to a person who is baptized: she is connected to Jesus and promised a new life. Pretty sweet, don't you think?

So if you haven't been baptized, you might want to think about it (as in, "Git 'r done"). And if you have done it or have had it done to you . . . um . . . you still ought to think about it (as in reflect on what God has done for you). Think about it.

See also: born again; forgiveness; repentance

Bible \BĪ-buhl\ n.

A book that Christians believe is so holy and inspired that they almost never read it for fear that it might draw them closer to God and neighbor or change their lives in some other inconvenient way.

Okay, if you want to get all technical, the Bible is not really a book; it is a library of books that are handily bound together in one cover. The Bible consists of two parts: the Old Testament and the New Testament. But you don't want to get all technical, do you?

Oh. In that case, this library of books contains many different kinds of writings, such as history books, poems, prayers, letters, parables, visions, prophetic messages, and so on. (We could go on, but we know you don't want to be *that* technical.) What's more, these many different books were written by many different people over the course of many centuries. Perhaps the oldest material in the Bible was written down about twelve centuries before Jesus was born, although it probably existed in the form of oral tradition before it was written down. You know what oral tradition is—that is what your father said about your mother when she wasn't around to correct him. The youngest material in the Bible was written less than one hundred years after Jesus—good grief, it was so young that it was barely legal to drive in most states.

The Bible is fully the inspired WORD OF GOD and also fully the word of human beings. It is not 50 percent Word of God and 50 percent word of human beings. It is not 100 percent Word of God and 0 percent word of human beings. It is not 0 percent Word of God and 100 percent word of human beings.

Yes, we know how crazy that sounds, but there it is. Think of it this way. Is a dollar bill paper or is it money? It is 100 percent both. Is it just paper that represents money? No. Is it just money that seems to look like paper? No. It is fully paper and fully money.

In the same way, the Bible is both the Word of God and the word of human beings. Here is the point. God is not so holy and so mighty that God has to remain far away and distant from us. God loves us and comes close to us. God's Word actually inhabits our words.

A story might help. A cynic once asked a Christian, "How big is your God?" The Christian replied, "God is so big that the vast universe cannot contain God and yet so small that God is able to dwell even in your meager heart." That's the way God's Word is, too. It is so vast that the entire creation cannot contain it and so small that it comes to us in the very small letters and words of the Bible.

B

See also: apocrypha; canon

bishop \BIH-shuhp\ n.

An overseer of Christians who can be pretty handy to have around—provided he or she remembers who actually died for our sins.

Don't get us wrong. We like bishops—we really do. Some of our best friends are bishops. But we are a postmodern group of writers, so we've been conditioned to question authority and to "stick it to da man." And, like it or not, Christian bishops have been *the* authority and "da man" for a long time (even when those bishops are women).

And here's a confusing thing. At different times and places and in different Christian traditions, what a bishop is and does has changed. In fact, some Christian groups don't even have bishops at all (but don't let them fool you, they still have authority and "da man"). Here are some examples:

- In New Testament times (1 Timothy 3:1–2; Titus 1:7; Philippians 1:1) and for the first few centuries of the church, bishops were really *lead pastors*, that is, pastors who oversaw the work of other pastors but still functioned as pastors of congregations. Some traditions, such as the African Methodist Episcopal (AME) Church, still follow this model.

- Later, bishops became administrators who oversaw the ministry of larger chunks of real estate called "dioceses" or "synods" in various traditions. Roman Catholics, Methodists, Episcopalians, and some Lutherans fit here.

- Later, some traditions eschewed (translation: canned) the office of bishop because the power of the office could get out of hand. These traditions still have an oversight office, they just call it something else: president, moderator, or grand poobah. Presbyterians, Baptists, and some Lutherans fit here.

In the end, pretty much every Christian group has needed an oversight office, whether they call it "bishop" or not. Overseeing the work of the church is godly work, and as with all godly works, it is important to remember that it is about God (not us).

See also: pastor/priest

blasphemy \BLA-sfuh-mee\ n.

If theology were butchery—and it often is—blasphemy would be the tools used to mar a sacred cow.

blaspheme \BLAS-feem\ v.

To apply soil to God's name with one's tongue.

If to utter a heresy is to speak something untrue or demeaning about God, to blaspheme is to do so intentionally, knowing that it is wrong but proclaiming it anyway. It's worth noting that blasphemy was the charge most often leveled at Jesus of Nazareth, whose radical forgiveness of sins—implying his equality with God because he claimed the authority to do something only God can do—really ticked off those who were sensibly religious. Christian faith is based on the most blasphemous assertion of all: on the cross, God suffered and died . . . for you.

See also: apostasy; heresy; sin

blessing \BLEH-seeng\ n.

The act or words by which one bestows favor on someone who certainly hasn't earned it but probably thinks they deserve it.

Sometimes words actually *do* something. Consider the difference between these two scenarios. (Legal disclaimer: all characters and situations are fictitious; any resemblance to our mothers, wives, or husbands is a complete coincidence.)

B

Scenario 1: It is Friday night, and your friends invite you out for pizza. You ask your spouse/parent. There is a slight pause after which the answer comes, *without enthusiasm*, "Go ahead."

Scenario 2: It is Friday night, and your friends invite you out for pizza. You ask your spouse/parent. There is a slight pause after which the answer comes, *with enthusiasm*, "Go ahead, and have a good time."

The difference between scenario 1 and scenario 2 (besides the fact that your chances of experiencing scenario 2 are better if your room is clean and you did the dishes) is that in scenario 1 you got *permission*, which means you can go, but you will pay for it later. In scenario 2, you got a blessing, which means that God's face has shone upon you.

God blesses us in two ways. First, God blesses us *directly* when God gives us undeserved gifts—a sunny day, a good friend, a rhubarb pie.

Second, God blesses us *indirectly* when we speak words or do actions that bless others. Consider this commonly used benediction: "May the Lord bless you and keep you, may the Lord's face shine upon you and be gracious to you, the Lord look upon you with favor and grant you peace."

Now, go and try it.

See also: grace

born again \BOHRN-uh-GEHN\ v., adj.

The process (v.) of reuterine expatriation; the state (adj.) of having been so expatriated.

To borrow from Kid Rock, to be born again is to come back with a little more love. The most common mistake regarding rebirth is to think that it has something to do with our own actions or is the product of our own doing. This is just as true of spiritual rebirth as it is of physical birth. To be born again is to live in the promise that is given in baptism. It takes the work of the Holy Spirit, and it is done for us.

See also: baptism; Holy Spirit; repentance

canon \ᴋᴀ-**nuhn**\ n.

Not to be confused with a large weapon (this canon only has one "n"), the canon is the list of books comprising the authoritative, written Word of God . . . which sinners often use as a large weapon to bombard each other.

Canon literally means "standard" or "measuring rod." If we stopped the conversation here, most of us would be confused and no better off. What does a ruler—such as a twelve-inch piece of wood—have to do with the Bible? At first glance, not much. But upon reflection, the notion of the *standard* collection of books that the church will recognize as the written Word of God is very important.

It took years to put the canon in place. (Some things never change with the church.) The books didn't gain authority overnight.

At the time of Jesus, a lot of Jewish writings were floating around, and not all of them were viewed as Scripture. Various Jewish groups had differing opinions about which Jewish writings were *canonical*. Pretty much every Jewish group was sold on the Torah (the first five books of the Bible). After some spirited—and Holy Spirit–led—debates, the Christian church and Rabbinic Judaism both came to accept the Prophets and the Writings (basically all the books from Joshua to Malachi in the Old Testament).

Nerd quotient: okay, if you want to get all technical, even today the various Christian traditions don't perfectly agree on which Old Testament (OT) books are canonical. Protestant churches have fol-lowed the Jewish list and recog-nize thirty-nine OT books. The Roman Catholic Church also acknowledges Tobit, Judith, the Wisdom of Solomon, Ecclesias-ticus, Baruch, the Letter of Jere-miah, and 1–2 Maccabees (aka the APOCRYPHA) as well as additions to Esther and Daniel. Orthodox Churches include all of the extra stuff that Catholics do and a few additional books . . . exactly which books depends on which Orthodox Church we are talking about.

But don't get worked up about these variations—in the big picture, the differences are very small. What we share in common is much bigger and more significant than what we don't share. Hey, that's true about life in general and not just the Bible, but we guess that's a sermon for another time . . . back to the Bible.

The New Testament (NT) canon is a simpler matter: all Christian groups agree on the twenty-seven books that make up the New Testament canon. Whew! As mentioned above, it took a while for all Christians to agree on the New Testament canon. Not until the fourth century (almost two-and-a-half centuries after the last New Testament book was written!) was the final list of the New Testament canon agreed upon. Here's a fun nugget of trivia: the author of this NT list was Athanasius, the bishop of Alexandria, Egypt. (You never know when you might have to whip that line out at a party.)

See also: apocrypha; Bible; Catholic; orthodox; Protestant

catholic \KATH-uh-lihk\ or \KATH-lihk\ adj.

A word meaning "universal," and therefore often used to describe only one part of the Christian family.

Catholic n.

A Christian who belongs to the Roman Catholic Church.

First of all, forget everything you think you know about the word *catholic*. Forget about Mass every Sunday, priests who can't marry, praying to the Virgin Mary, the well-dressed old dude who lives at the Vatican, sweetly clad-in-plaid children going to private schools, fish on Fridays, and so on. Just forget it.

The word *catholic* actually means "universal." From very early in the history of the church, the term referred to the belief that even though the church is made up of many, many, many congregations, in many, many, many cities, in many, many, many countries, the church is still *universal*.

C

Every Christian may belong to a local congregation, but every Christian also shares in a fellowship with every other Christian in the *universe*. The church is a miracle that is made possible by the power of the Holy Spirit. Our *catholicity* (now there is a word to impress your friends and relatives) is a gift from God, not something that we do achieve, can achieve, or are expected to achieve.

The church is not limited by geography, race, language, culture, style of worship, or gender (see Galatians 3:28). The church is open to all and includes all who follow Christ.

So what about those Christians who claim the name Catholic for themselves? Yep, they are part of the universal church. And so are you.

See also: church; orthodox; Protestant

Christ (Messiah) \krīst\ \muh-sī-uh\ n.

Jesus's official title (but not his last name); the one promised to rescue and rule humanity, even though humanity had no idea that it needed rescuing and ruling.

Alright, let's start with the language stuff. *Christ* is from the Greek word *christos*, meaning "anointed one." *Christos* matches up with the Hebrew word *mashiach*, which also means "anointed one." So look at you, language expert!

You might wonder what anointing has to do with Jesus. The answer: a whole lot. In the Old Testament, the "anointed one" (*mashiach*, *christos*) was the one chosen by God to be king in Jerusalem and rule over God's people. Why did they call him (it was always a him) the anointed one? Because they dumped perfumed oil all over the poor guy! Check out 1 Samuel 16 to find out how David got oil poured on him when God selected him to be king. Why dump oils on your royals, you ask? Maybe so that they would absorb vitality and power into the skin? Maybe so they didn't stink as much as everyone else? The reasons are fuzzy.

God's chosen king, God's anointed one (*Messiah, Christ*) was supposed to rule over the people wisely and justly. But as you know, power corrupts, and the power given to the kings of Israel absolutely corrupted them. These kings were for the most part a lousy bunch. Even the best of them, like David, Solomon, Hezekiah, and Josiah, were less than perfect. Also, they all died.

Finally, Israel's monarchy collapsed altogether when Jerusalem fell to the Babylonians in 587 BCE. But a thread of a promise began to develop. The prophets began to tell of a new ruler who would establish a kingdom of unending peace (see, for instance, Isaiah 9). The people of Israel imagined that this ultimate Messiah (Christ) would be an awesome king like David but even more awesome still! This messiah would be the final messiah; he would rescue God's people from all oppressors and make Israel great again.

So around the time Jesus was born, expectations were high. Surely God would soon be sending the once-and-for-all anointed one! Jesus was not an obvious first choice. He matched some of the expectations—descended from David, born in Bethlehem, wise, compassionate, righteous—but not all. True, he was hailed as a king when he went up to Jerusalem, but it went downhill from there. Instead of kicking out the Roman occupiers, he told Pilate, "My kingdom is not of this world." Instead of a crown of jewels, he wore a crown of thorns. Instead of a royal throne, he was hung on a cross. The sign above his head mocked him as a king. He was anointed with sweet-smelling oil, but only to prepare his body for burial.

The Bible proclaims Jesus as the Anointed One, the Messiah, and the Christ, but in an "Opposite Day" kind of way. Jesus is not your run-of-the-mill ruler—amassing riches, enforcing laws, making wars, and so on. Instead, this Christ—whose strength is perfected in weakness—rules in a new way, through grace, mercy, and love. Amen. Mic drop.

See also: Christology; God; gospel; Holy Spirit; Jesus; Son of God

Christian \KRIS-chihn\ n.

A person so valuable that the Son of God died for them but so worthless that they cannot save themselves; a person who follows Jesus Christ, at least insofar as Christ's teachings are not inconsistent with a life of continued sinning.

The word *Christian* was first meant as an insult . . . and if you have known many Christians, you know why. Christians are no different than other people. They are sinners. They might mean to do well but fail. They might mean to do you ill and succeed. They might not care if they do you well or ill because they might just not care. And if you put them together in a group, they will fight over the stupidest things you can possibly imagine: the style of the church's entryway, whether women have a right to vote at church meetings to decide on the style of the church's entryway, whether churches should have meetings to vote about whether women can vote . . . you get the idea.

As we say, *in and of themselves*, Christians are no different than any other people—they're sinners. But Christians have one thing that makes them completely different—Christians have Jesus Christ.

Now we have to be pretty careful when we say that "Christians have Jesus Christ." Christians don't possess or own Jesus. Rather, Christians know that they have a safe place to which they can flee from every EVIL; Jesus is that place. When we say, "Christians have Jesus Christ," it is like saying that a screaming baby in his mother's arms "has his mother."

Another way to put this is to say that a Christian is someone whose life has been claimed by the risen Lord Jesus Christ.

A Christian is *not* a better person than someone of another religion. Rather, a Christian is someone who has been claimed by the only truly perfect person ever to live. A Christian is *not* someone who has a better, stronger, or deeper faith than someone of another religion. Rather, what matters about a Christian is who they place their FAITH in—Jesus. A Christian is *not* someone who worships more fervently, prays more sincerely, or has a richer spiritual life. A Christian is one who worships Jesus, prays in Jesus's name, and whose spiritual life depends on and is centered fully on the GRACE of Jesus Christ.

St. Paul spoke to a group of Christians this way: "Not many of you were wise according to human standards, not many were powerful, not many were of noble birth. But God chose what is foolish in the world to shame the wise; God chose what is weak in the world to shame the strong, God chose what is low and despised in the world" (1 Corinthians 1:26–28).

There you have it: In the eyes of the world, Christians are not wise— they are foolish; they are not powerful—they are weak; they are not well-born—they are lowly and despised.

But get this. God loves everyone in the world so much that God was willing to send the only Son, Jesus Christ, to suffer and die for us. God even loves the fools, the weak, and the lowly enough to send Jesus to die for them. And that is what a Christian is—a person who knows they are worth much in the eyes of the world but knows that in the eyes of God, they are worth dying for.

See also: atonement; Christ (Messiah); church; Jesus

Christology \krih-STAH-luh-jee\ n.

Crazy talk about Christ.

By now you've probably figured out that THEOLOGY involves lots of made-up words to describe simple concepts. This is no different. Christology basically involves putting everything about Jesus Christ—his person, his work, his dental plan—under the proverbial microscope and trying to understand its minutiae. This involves everything from how much of him is human versus divine, what he did versus what he does, who he was then versus who he is to you now. Believe it or not, things can get a little tricky.

Maybe you noticed that there are lots of ways to be Christian. That's because lots of people have a different Christology—in other words, they understand Jesus a little differently. There are many shades of belief regarding what Jesus's death and resurrection meant, what his teachings mean, and even whether he thought women were okay. Since Jesus was the impetus for the formation of the Christian faith, even the tiniest details can make an enormous difference.

That's why Christology has spawned books, courses, and schisms. For individuals, churches, denominations, and indeed the entire Christian faith, it's important to get straight who Jesus was and what he means. On the surface it's a straightforward concept—but have you ever really read some of the stuff Jesus said in the Bible or the Bible says about him? It's no wonder people argue about him all the time.

See also: Christ (Messiah); Jesus; heresy

church \chuhrch\ n.

The people whom God has formed—like Adam in the book of Genesis—out of the mud, muck, and mire of human nature.

C

Groucho Marx famously quipped, "I would not join any club that would have someone like me for a member." Pretty much, the church is that club—except that the church isn't a club; it is a mission. More on that later.

The church can be hard to define, so we'll proceed by process of elimination. The church is not: a club of like-minded people (or a club of likeable people, for that matter); a beautiful building with ornate architecture, stained glass, and an organ; a not-for-profit corporation for God's will; a denomination such as Lutherans, Catholics, and so on.

So what is the church? The church is a people. But can we be more specific?

Again, we'll work by process of elimination. The church is not: a group of people who share a system of belief, worship, or faith practices; a group of people who are holier or more righteous than the rest of the world (as Holden Caulfield might have said, this idea would make good ol' Jesus puke); a group of people who are more spiritual than others.

So what is the church? The church is the assembly of forgiven sinners.

C

Back to Groucho Marx. The church is the people no respectable and sane person would want to be a part of: sinners, every last one of them. As Paul reminded the church in Corinth, "Not many of you were wise by human standards, not many were powerful, not many were of noble birth" (1 Corinthians 1:26). In other words, not the dean's list, the varsity, or the prosperous.

The church is God's creation, not something formed by the agreement or actions of human beings—hence it is called the body of Christ, not the body of losers. Note how God's action is key in the definition of the church in the ancient creeds, which describe the church as one, holy, catholic, and apostolic:

- The *oneness* of the church refers to the fact that although the church always disagrees and divides, God keeps it spiritually united under the one Christ.
- The *holiness* of the church refers to the fact that although the church is full of sinners, God forgives them and makes them holy.
- The *catholicity* (that means "universality") of the church refers to the fact that although human beings set up churchly institutions that are specific to time and place, God unites the church in all ages and places.
- The church is APOSTOLIC (meaning "sent") because although it is always turning in on itself and serving its own needs, God is always at work sending it out into the world as part of God's mission to save, love, and bless the world.

And this mission, after all, is why the church exists. In fact, the church doesn't *have* a mission; the church *is* a mission. The church is part of God's reaching out to love, save, and bless all of creation.

See almost every article in this book but especially: apostle; apostolic literature; evangelism; gospel; holy & holiness; justification; pastor/ priest; simultaneously saint and sinner

communion \kuh-MYOO-nyuhn\ n.

The ritual eating and drinking of bread and wine that is so holy that many believers participate by just going through the motions—the body and blood of Christ in, with, and under the bread and wine.

Synonyms: Lord's Supper; Holy Communion; Eucharist, the; Mass, the; sacrament of the table; foretaste of the feast to come.

The word *communion* literally refers to the act of sharing things in common, of participating together, of coming together. And ever since Jesus Christ initiated the sacrament of Holy Communion, Christians have been coming together to argue about what Holy Communion is. They have been participating together in a long history of bitter disagreements and divisions over the meaning of the sacrament.

This ironic history of bitter disagreements over the Lord's Supper teaches us one central thing about the sacrament: it is not what we humans do in the sacrament that matters but rather the actions that God does. *What we do* is basically meaningless because compared with the burning sun of what God does, our little candlelight actions are simply outshined.

So what does God do in Holy Communion? Let's roll the video tape.

"While they were eating, Jesus took a loaf of bread, and after blessing it he broke it, gave it to the disciples, and said, 'Take, eat; this is my body.' Then he took a cup, and after giving thanks he gave it to them, saying, 'Drink from it, all of you; for this is my blood of the covenant, which is poured out for many for the forgiveness of sins'" (Matthew 26:26–28).

This passage narrates the last supper, during which Jesus instituted Holy Communion. Notice what the passage says God does in Holy Communion:

- *Forgiving sins.* As we eat the bread and drink the wine, God speaks this promise to us: I am forgiving your sins . . . right now . . . in these words . . . your sins are forgiven.
- *Being present.* As we eat the bread and drink the wine, God speaks this promise to us: I am present with you right now . . . really, truly present . . . I am here.
- *Uniting us.* As we eat the bread and drink the wine, God speaks this promise to us: You are all one, you are united by my Spirit . . . even though you think you are divided . . . even though you disagree and sin . . . you are one.

To repeat: God does these things. We cannot do them for ourselves, so in the Lord's Supper, the Lord does them for us.

So what *do we do* in the Supper? Well, we do the only thing a person does when a promise is made: we believe. Sure, we can do things to focus our minds—like praying or concentrating—to decrease the chances that we just go through the motions. But the basic nature of the Supper is that it is a promise. The only way to take part in a promise is to believe it: "I forgive you . . . I am with you . . . I am making you one."

See also: baptism; means of grace; sacrament

community \kuh-MYOO-nih-tee\ n.

That group (and the sense of belonging that comes with it) you would crave to be a part of, if it weren't so full of people.

As the old sitcom jingle goes, "Sometimes you wanna go where everybody knows your name." Of course, the problem with that is that they know pretty much everything else too, like how you smell, what your oh-so-sensitive areas are, how to get your goat, and where you keep your skeletons buried. But the good thing about communities is that they *are* so full of people— people just like us.

When community is what it's supposed to be, we know that we belong. We are accepted as we are, protected, loved, and encouraged to grow in our own faith and love.

See also: church

confession \kuhn-FEH-shuhn\ n.

Religious diarrhea of the mouth.

C

confessional \kuhn-FEH-shuh-nuhl\ n.

A place where one may apologize for having, on occasion, not run properly at the mouth (and also many and other various sins and failings).

confessional \kuhn-FEH-shuh-nuhl\ adj.

Those whose mouths run freely, with praise, thanksgiving, prayer, and witness.

The word *confession* has fallen on hard times. Today when you hear "confession" you think either about a criminal who has owned up to her crime or about a penitent spilling out his sins to a priest. But there's way more to confession than this. Confession is the expression of what you believe, as in "confession of faith." The key, central, chief, foremost confession of faith for Christians is "Jesus is Lord." According to the Bible, "No one can say 'Jesus is Lord' except by the Holy Spirit" (1 Corinthians 12:3). Furthermore, confession of faith is often accompanied by a promise. "If you confess with your mouth that Jesus is Lord and believe in your heart that God raised him from the dead, you will be saved" (Romans 10:9).

A lot of times we may wish that people who share their faith would keep it to themselves. Especially in confined spaces.

And here's the deal: if you are going to confess your faith, you had better know it, at least a little. But it's nothing to be afraid of; it isn't rocket science, after all. If you want to be a daring Christian and confess what you believe about God, Jesus, and the Holy Spirit, start with what you know. What has God done for you? What is God up to in your life? And what do you know about God that you think you just couldn't live without? And just go from there.

Note: Over the centuries Christians have drafted official confessions. For example, the Nicene Creed (325 CE) is the central confession defining Trinitarian Christians.

See also: apologetics; creed; doctrine; witness

contrition \kuhn-TRIH-shuhn\ n.

The rare spiritual condition of feeling intensely sorry—being sorry that you gave away your last cookie doesn't count.

Aka REPENTANCE, remorse, regret, compunction, sorrow, penitence—gosh we've got a lot of words for this, don't we? *Contrition* is a state of the heart—if we are sorry for what we have done or failed to do, said or failed to say, thought or failed to think (you get the idea), contrition is the intention and then following through that sets things right. Cont*rite* (adj.) is the opposite of cont*wrong*. We can't do it ourselves; we need the Holy Spirit's help to do it.

See also: forgiveness; repentance

council \KOWN-tsuhl\ n.

A huddle of the church's bishops for the sake of solving some puzzle that was probably caused by one or more bishops.

A *council* is the churchy version of a stockholders meeting, called to mediate a crisis in the body of Christ. Councils have made judgments on issues ranging from the accepted books of the Bible to offering official rulings on doctrines and heresies to deciding on issues of church governance. Have you noticed that this article is boring? That's because councils are boring. Early in the church, seven councils were held that almost all Christians today recognize as authoritative: Nicea (325), Constantinople I (381), Ephesus (431), Chalcedon (451), Constantinople II (553), Constantinople III (680–81), and Nicea II (787).

See also: church; doctrine; heresy

covenant \KUH-vuh-nuhnt\ n.

How God does—and does not—maintain a relationship with humanity.

We are going to make this simple, since some people are a little slow. To have a covenant (which means a sacred contract or deal), you have to have these things:

- Two parties (not as in celebrations, but as in two people or groups of people—hello!)
- A set of promises
- A sign (that is, some sign so that you know you are party to the covenant)

C

Why does it matter that you know this? Because the covenant is one of the major ways of understanding how God interacts and maintains relationships with people. In the Old Testament there are four major covenants. And the New Testament is the story of God's covenant to save all creation. So here is a little chart that might help you along.

Maybe you noticed we said that covenant both is and is not the way that God deals with us. Here's the deal. Covenant is the way that God deals with us because in these covenants, God makes promises. And God always keeps promises unconditionally. But covenant is also not the way that God deals with us, since each of these covenants expects human beings to be faithful to God and "keep the covenant." And do you know what? Humanity never holds up its end of the deal. And God still keeps promises. Unconditionally.

C

COVENANT	THE PARTIES	THE PROMISE(S)	THE SIGN
Noah	God and all flesh	God would never again destroy the earth via a flood	Rainbow
Abraham	God, Abraham, and Sarah's descendants	Abraham's descendants would be a great nation and a blessing to the earth	Male circumcision
Moses	God and the nation of Israel	"I will be your God and you will be my people"	The sabbath day
David	God and David's descendants	God would protect Jerusalem and one of David's descendants would forever reign over Israel	(No sign; this is the proverbial exception that proves the rule. But you demand a sign? Think of the temple as the sign)
New Covenant	God and all humanity	Forgiveness of sins, eternal life, meaning in life, God's guidance, blessing, and so on	Baptism in the name of the Father, Son, and Holy Spirit

It's important to recognize that in each situation, *God* initiates and upholds the covenant—definitely not the people. Thank goodness we have a God who exceeds our expectations and never gives up. Thank goodness God is patient and keeps promises.

And thank goodness that God has made promises to you: you are a child of God, a child of the covenant, someone whom God loves, someone God is calling to join in God's mission to love, save, and bless the world.

See also: forgiveness; grace; promise

creation \kree-Ā-shuhn\ n.

God's once-upon-a-time and still-at-it work of bringing stuff into existence, which may or may not include that thing growing in the back of your fridge.

You know how creative types are. Finicky, temperamental, difficult, sometimes a bit prima donna–ish. Can you imagine God hanging out before anything existed saying, "I just can't work in this environment; how can I be expected to be creative with such dull surroundings? I want light! I want sky! I want air! I want water! I want plants! I want animals! I want people! I want a 1970 000-18 Martin guitar!"

And just like that, there they were: light, sky, air, water, plants, animals, people. (The Martin took a while longer, but trust us—it was worth the wait.)

Creation is such an important topic in the Bible that many passages are dedicated to it. Just check out Genesis 1–2; Psalm 8; 19; and 104; Job 38–41; Proverbs 8:22–31; and John 1:1–4. A pastor friend of ours was put on trial by his church for not believing exactly what his church group wanted him to believe about creation. No, we are not kidding, church people suck sometimes—see the articles on SIN, CHURCH, and HERESY. Anyway, he was asked, "What do you believe about how the world was created?" They wanted him to say, "I believe the world was created in six twenty-four-hour days." Instead he said, "I believe exactly what the Bible says about creation." His point? There are lots of biblical passages about creation, not just one passage. You can't measure the biblical view of creation with a stopwatch.

So what does the Bible say about creation? Here are some basics.

Who. The Bible is clear on who created everything. The One God—Father, Son, and Holy Spirit. A sub-point here is that creation and God are separate—God is in all creation, but creation is not God. We don't worship frogs or hills, but the maker of the frogs and hills.

When and how. Once-and-for-all and still-happening. Try this: Read Genesis 1 and make a list of all the things that God created directly (with no help—such as the earth in v. 9) and of all the things that God created indirectly (for example, God uses the earth to "bring forth" plants [v. 11] and animals [v. 24]). The point? Creation happened once but is still happening. After all, God created you indirectly through your parents!

Why. Here is a question that science cannot answer. Why does creation exist? The Bible says that God created everything for the sake of goodness and for the sake of love. Psalm 104 says that God even created some creatures, like Leviathan, for the fun of it, to laugh at! Ha. Maybe God made your little brother with that red hair and big ears because God needed a good laugh.

But we are not suggesting that science cannot answer a lot of questions that the Bible can't! We need science. Desperately. Science is the joyful study of God's creation. The Bible is not a science textbook, nor does it claim to be. Science and theology need each other.

See also: creature; image of God; Trinity

creature \KREE-cher\ n.

An idea that counters and balances the idea that you are in charge of the universe.

When asked by a customs agent if he had anything to declare, Oscar Wilde is reported to have said, "I have nothing to declare but my own genius." When he won the heavyweight boxing title, Muhammad Ali shouted, "I'm the king of the world." And the Beatles' member John Lennon remarked, "We're more popular than Jesus."

Our point? Human beings tend to forget that we are *creatures.* That is, we didn't create ourselves. Our Creator doesn't mind if we celebrate our triumphs, but perhaps we owe at least a humble foot-note that might acknowledge that we didn't get here on our own.

See also: creation

creed \kreed\ n.

Not to be confused with the boxer who pummeled Rocky Balboa, a personal statement of belief, written by someone else, for use in pummeling heretics.

Related to the Latin word *credo*, which means "I believe," a creed can refer either to one's personal beliefs or to an official summary of Christian beliefs, often available in pseudo-poetic form. The Apostles', Nicene, and Athanasian creeds were hammered out in the early ecumenical councils of the church. While they do give voice to official teachings of the faith, the church is not at its best when it persecutes people who believe things counter to the creeds.

See also: confession; council; faith

cross \krahs\ n.

An instrument of torture, which the Savior wore on his back in order to save us from our sins—which we, in turn, wear on our fronts as gilded, sparkling, gold-plated, jewel-encrusted expressions of faith.

Lots of folks wear a cross as fashion *excessory* (and no, that's not a typo). But the cross was an instrument of torture and death, and wearing one isn't about looking good. The cross is where Jesus went to die so that you might have abundant, eternal life. The cross is about salvation, not fashion sense. It shouldn't matter if it matches your pumps. The cross is the decisive thing that Jesus did and endured for you.

The cross reminds us of what God is really like and how God works. What's God like? God is not what we expect. God is like a poor baby, born of a virgin in a barn. God is like a criminal, tortured to death and abandoned by friends. How does God work? God works through the lowest, most despised people. God finds us in our lowest moments, by working through the most unexpected folks.

See also: Christ (Messiah); grace; Jesus

curse \kuhrs\ n.

Not the ~~seven~~ three words you can't say on television but what you really wish on someone you don't much care for.

A curse involves wishing someone the absolute worst thing(s) possible. More than just that, it involves saying that worst thing out loud and with intent. Words matter; words actually do something. And curses are intended to do harm.

There is a story in the book of Numbers about when the people of Israel are on their way to the promised land. The king of Moab, a joker called Balak, wasn't too keen on the idea. So Balak went to a prophet by the name of Balaam and paid him a huge chunk of change to pronounce a curse against Israel and stop them from coming. Balaam did as he was told (and actually what God told him to go ahead and do), but instead of curse words, God made words of blessing come out of Balaam's mouth. (That probably made actual curse words come out of Balak's yapper and got his mouth washed out with soap.)

And that's what we get from Jesus. Jesus is God's Word of blessing spoken to all of humankind. And Jesus came to counter any and all curses with his blessing. As the great advent hymn puts it, "He comes to make his blessings flow, far as the curse is found."

See also: blessing; gospel

death \dehth\ n.

Dresses in black, carries a long-handled scythe; the last enemy to be defeated.

Perhaps you know the type. Death never gives up, even though it's the fourth quarter and death is way behind. The home team, coached by the Father, quarterbacked by the Son, inspired by the Spirit, is ahead 77–0. But death— the enemy, the opponent—never gives up. He won't admit that the battle is over, the victory is won.

"The last enemy to be destroyed is death. . . . Thanks be to God, who gives us the victory through our Lord Jesus Christ" (1 Corinthians 15:26, 57).

See also: heaven; promise; salvation

D

Decalogue \DEH-kuh-lahg\ n.

Eight big no-no's and two impossible demands. Alternatively, God's record label.

Synonym: The Ten Commandments

Only the Greek language can take a clunky three-word buffalo like "The Ten Commandments" and transform it into the sleek and ultra-cool zinger *Decalogue*. It's like compacting a three-hour

Cecil B. DeMille epic into a kick-butt, ninety-minute indie remake. Impress your friends (at least your linguist-geek friends): say *Decalogue.*

If you've ever seen a painting of Moses holding the Ten Commandments, you'll remember that he was holding *two* stone tablets (see Exodus 31:18). Five commandments on each tablet, right? *Wrong!* The commandments are not divided up five and five but according to those commandments that apply to our relationship with God on the one hand (or tablet) and with our neighbors on the other hand (or tablet).

Relating to God: no other gods, don't worship idols, don't misuse God's name, and keep the Sabbath. Relating to your neighbor: honor your parents; don't kill, commit adultery, steal, bear false witness, covet, or covet (there are two coveting rules; coveting must be easy to do and hard not to do). Find the complete original list in Exodus 20, Deuteronomy 5, or your denomination's standard catechism.

D

Note that a relationship with God is not dependent on successfully executing one, six, or even all of the commandments but on God's grace alone.

See also: covenant; law; law, uses of the; neighbor; sin

discernment \dih-SUHRN-muhnt\ n.

Not to be confused with dis-urn-ment, the process by which you emptied Aunt Linda's ashes into the planters at the mall, the act of figuring out what in the world God wants you to do.

Okay. Listen up now.

We mean it. Listen! Up! *Listen! Up!* Literally! Since heaven is figuratively up, we want you to literally listen figuratively up.

That's what discernment is all about. Listening to God.

Ever wonder what direction God is leading you? Ever want some help solving a tough situation? Ever have a tantalizing offer and wonder whether to accept it?

D

If you have, you've been in need of discernment—the act of listening for God's will. The best ways to do this are to pray, to read Scripture, and to consult with your Spiritual Board of Advisors—that is, your trusted friends and mentors in your community of faith.

Which Aunt Linda did, when she discerned that she wanted to spend eternity where she was happiest—at the mall.

disciple \dih-sī-puhl\ n. *(but sometimes v.)*

A person who follows Jesus, who is, of course, pursuing us.

Child: Mom, I want to go to the party—my best friend is going.

Mom: If your best friend were jumping off a bridge, would you follow?

Child: Mom, you want me to follow Jesus, right? And Jesus said, "Take up your CROSS and follow me," but Jesus got himself crucified, so do you really want me to follow Jesus?

Mom: You have a point—you can go to the party.

Child: Really?

Mom: No. And I still want you to follow Jesus, but don't get yourself crucified before I have grandkids.

What is a disciple? A disciple is a person who follows someone. A *Christian disciple* follows Jesus. And there is the rub. You are actually called to follow someone who gave his life away for the sake of the world. What's up with that?

Well, two things are up with that. First, to follow Jesus means believing and trusting that Jesus always loves you, always forgives you, is always chasing after you, and will never ever give up on you. To be a disciple of Jesus is to know that you are the one sheep out of a hundred that is lost and that Jesus will never rest until you are back in the sheep pen. Don't believe us? Well, don't believe us, believe the Bible—read the parable of the lost sheep in Luke 15:1–7. The point of the story is that even sinners matter to Jesus. It teaches us that to be a disciple is to know that Jesus was willing to suffer on the cross *for you!*

There is a second side to being a disciple. To follow Jesus also means that we follow him in his mission to chase after all of those other lost sheep. (Or is it sheeps? Never mind—in the end, it's mutton either way.) But we do know this. We follow the One who chases after the lost, the sinners, and the wounded. And that means in addition to knowing that Jesus is always chasing after us, we follow him as he is chasing after others—and that in turn means that we are always chasing after the lost, the sinners, and the wounded.

Don't believe us? Don't believe us, believe the Bible! Read the parable of the lost sheep again but this time in Matthew 18:10–14. Notice that Jesus tells the same story, but this time the point is that everyone who follows Jesus is to never give up chasing after the one lost sheep.

So being a disciple involves always knowing that Jesus is on a mission *to us*—to love us, to save us, and to bless us. And being a disciple involves always knowing that we follow Jesus on this mission and that Jesus is on a mission *through us*—to love through us, to save through us, and to bless through us.

See also: Christian; service

doctrine \DAHK-trihn\ n.

The fine line between theological sanity and insanity.

There is a fine line between being crazy and being crazy like a fox. Is Uncle Charlie a complete whack job, or is he just creative? When it comes to crazy (or creative) talk about God, doctrines are those chalk lines that form the boundaries between creative and crazy.

For example, the doctrine of creation says, "God created everything thing that exists." A non-doctrinal teaching (a HERESY) teaches, "Everything that exists is God."

For some, doctrines are annoying and problematic, cramping the style of creative thinkers. After all, who's to say that continual reincarnation can't be part of good Christian faith? (Well, the Bible, for one.) But this is where the rules and guidelines simply help us understand who we are and what mistakes not to repeat. Like most things, if there's a rule about it, it probably means someone tried it to very bad results.

Furthermore, doctrine helps answer questions that recur throughout time. Instead of each new believer having to map those boundaries between crazy and creative, doctrines pass on the wisdom of earlier generations. Not only does this save us trouble, but it helps ensure that all of us are on the same page.

See also: blasphemy; confession; dogma; heresy

dogma \DAWG-muh\ n.

Similar to doctrine, except turned up to eleven; those doctrines that are more equal than others.

Dogma, as everyone knows, is a movie starring Ben Affleck and Matt Damon that presents a view of faith completely contrary to Christian dogma. A dogma is an official church teaching that is considered more certain and central than run-of-the-mill doctrines. To reject a dogma is not only to throw the baby out with the bathwater but to assert that the baby isn't really a baby. A dogma is a doctrine that has been inspected, approved, and stamped "Grade A" by the church.

See also: doctrine; heresy

ecclesiology \eh-KLEE-zee-AH-luh-jee\ n.

The ultimate form of spiritual group navel gazing.

The church is the body of Christ. And like every other body, at some point, the body of Christ decided to ask, "Who am I? Why

am I here? How did I get here? Decaf or regular?" The church's self-reflection is called *ecclesiology* (from the Greek word *ecclesia*, meaning "assembly"). The aim is to consider the identity, nature, and function of the church. Like all navel gazing, the danger with ecclesiology is that it can become so self-reflective that the church loses its focus on God or starts to think that it is God.

See also: church

election \ee-LEHK-shuhn\ n.

The concept that membership in God's family is a selection process in which only one person—God—has a vote.

God works by choosing people—as disciples, as servants, as instruments of God's will. But one gets the impression that when doing this choosing, God is not very picky. God has a penchant for electing the least fit, least likely, and least worthy to accomplish God's plans: Abraham and Sarah (who gave up on God's promises), Jacob (cheater), Rahab (prostitute), David (adulterer/murderer), Peter, Paul, and Mary (awesome folk musicians, but also a denier, oppressor, and pregnant single girl, respectively). Not exactly Ivy-League material, but God chose them and used them.

It is human nature to think that we should have a vote about who God chooses. We think we know better than God who God should choose as servants, apostles, and ministers. We think God should choose the best, the purest, or those with most potential. Moses (a murderer) was so sure that he knew who God should choose that he spent two chapters of Exodus explaining to the burning bush why he shouldn't have been chosen! But God did, and God used Moses to free the people from slavery.

"Election" is really just another way to say that God is completely free—God is the only one who has a vote when it comes to who is in God's family and who God will use to save, love, and bless the world. In the same way, through baptism, God has elected you, blessed you, and given you a job to do.

See also: creation; creature; free will; omni-[fill in the blank], predestination

epiphany \ih-PIHF-uh-nee\ n.

When the light goes on.

Did you ever have a sudden realization that changed everything? Like when it first dawned on you that the whole Santa thing was based on works righteousness? Or when you finally figured out that the Minnesota Vikings were *never* going to win the Super Bowl? (You see what we did there? By putting it in print and italicizing the word "never," we more or less dared the football gods to prove us wrong.)

In the church, epiphany refers to the sudden, glorious, wow-we-didn't-see-that-coming, this-changes-everything revelation that God has come to us in Jesus Christ—born of a woman, crucified, and risen. Epiphany even gets its own special day—a day many Christians around the world celebrate on the thirteenth day of Christmas. Also known as Three Kings Day, Epiphany celebrates the dawning of glorious light on those magi who followed a star to the newborn king. So sing along with us: "We three kings of orient are . . . " How does the rest of it go again?

See also: incarnation; Jesus; revelation

eschatology \eh-skuh-TAH-luh-jee\ n.

The study of the way things get worse before they get better when all reality ends.

Those who make a career of speculating about "the end times" are theological proctologists—interested in how everything will come out. Who can help but love such excited and hopeful people? Eschatology is the study of theories about the end times. Good eschatology helps make sense of the present in light of what we know about how God wants things to end. Bad eschatology reads the Bible's verses as if they are tea leaves, trying to learn from them what Jesus says no one knows except God—when it will happen, and who will be saved (see Matthew 24:36).

See also: history; hope; rapture; salvation

ethics \EH-thihks\ n.

What you make of life from the leftovers after the main course of salvation has been served.

The Bible often describes salvation as a banquet, a feast of unparalleled joy (see Luke 15:11–32; 14:15–24; Matthew 22:1–14; 25:1–13;

John 2:1–12). We like the image in part because we love to eat and in part because the image speaks so powerfully about the communal nature of God's family. And we're pretty sure that the main course will be roast beef with Yorkshire pudding, and the dessert will be rhubarb pie.

E

But this image also helps us understand that pesky little thing known as *ethics*. Think of it like this: God is throwing *the* party of salvation. You are invited. So, having been raised well by your parents, you politely ask God, "What can I bring? A salad? How about a dessert? I make a mean rhubarb pie. Can I chip in for the expenses?"

And God says, "You don't have to bring a thing, I've got the whole thing under control. There's more than enough for everybody. And when I say *everybody*, I mean *everybody*. My son does this really cool thing with loaves and fishes."

And you say, "But can't I do anything?"

So God says, "Well, since I've covered everything to do with the feast, why don't you do something with the leftovers. The big dishes are all paid for, prepared, and plated. You can't even help with the clean up. But there is the matter of after. Why don't you take the leftovers and serve them to your neighbor?"

And that, friends, is what ethics is all about. Ethics is the matter of what we do with our lives in light of the fact that everything that matters has already been done for us. Ethics is reflecting upon right and wrong, good and evil, and what creation and our neighbor need the most from us.

You want to know more? Here are a couple of ten-dollar words with which you can impress friends and neighbors. On the one hand, some people think about ethics in a *teleological* way. From the Greek word *telos*, meaning "goal," this kind of ethical reflection starts at the end and says, "We decide if an action is right by reflecting on the results of the act." On the other hand, some people think about ethics in a *deontological* way. From the Greek word *deon*, meaning "duty" (or "flashy football player"), this kind of ethical reflection starts in the middle and says, "We decide if an action is right by thinking about whether the action itself is good or bad."

Had enough? We thought so. But since you've had enough, please serve up the leftovers to your neighbor.

See also: love; neighbor; sanctification

evangelical \eh-vuhn-JEH-lih-kuhl\ n., adj.

Describing an individual, institution or message that bears good news about Jesus, often and unfortunately in a strident fashion, the gist of which sadly is, "I'm okay, but you're pooched."

The word *evangelical* is derived from the Greek word *euangelion*, translated as "good news" or "GOSPEL." It both describes the content of what one preaches and the manner in which one does it. The content of the message is that Christ loves you just the way you are. The manner of the message is that you better become just like me, or I won't believe that you are saved.

As a term used to describe Christians, *evangelical* is again about the content—usually adopted by organizations that desire to be mission- or witness-oriented (often in spite of much evidence to the contrary)—and again about the manner in which the message is delivered—usually in a fashion by which a person suggests their own spiritual superiority by showing undue concern for another's immortal soul, talks over-much about God and Jesus, and just can't keep their noses out of our business.

In the New Testament only Philip is called *the* evangelist (Acts 21:8), perhaps due to his work with that Ethiopian dude or with the disciple Nathanael (cf. Acts 8; John 1:46). But Paul tells his student Timothy that he is to "do the work of *an* evangelist," which is to "proclaim the message," to "convince, rebuke and encourage" (2 Timothy 4:1–5)—and to do so in a manner consistent with the message!

So to be evangelical is both to be shaped by the good news—that God so loved the world, and so on—and to then share the story of Jesus with others.

See also: apologetics; apostle; mission; witness

evangelism \ee-VAN-juh-lih-zuhm\ v.

The terrifying act of sharing the good news with those who desperately need to hear it.

Evangelism is any act of speaking or doing that shares with others the good news that Jesus Christ loves them unconditionally. For most, evangelism describes an act that is presumptuous, pushy, and painful. But the Greek word *euangelion* means "good news." Evangelism is not a program or a strategy; it is a way of life, which is, of course, more confusing than Greek words.

See also: apologetics; evangelical; witness

evil \EE-vuhl\ n.

That which is not good; frequently the byproduct of good intentions.

Evil is a course of study, something that we can come to know (copyright Genesis 3:5) with surprising ease. Doctorates are available, but no special enrollment is needed to obtain a minor in evil studies.

Evil has traditionally been separated into two basic kinds: *moral* evil, which are the actions (or the attitudes that lead to them) performed by people, and *natural* evil, which consists of naturally occurring catastrophes—tornadoes, earthquakes, and visiting in-laws. Moral evil is closer to true evil—that which is wicked, immoral, malevolent; natural evil is closer to "bad"—that which is inconvenient, dreadful, and troubling, and which often provides the opportunity for moral evil. To moral and natural evil, the discerning palate will add a third, more specialized evil—the repugnance that is the *strawberry*-rhubarb pie. As it is written, "Let no strawberry be seen in the vicinity of the piecrust that has been set aside for rhubarb, lest the baker be cut off from in front of the stove." We're pretty sure it's in Leviticus somewhere.

Another helpful distinction is between "big" and "little" evil. Let's face it; most of us don't have what it takes to be totally, irreconcilably evil. We lack the guts, commitment, endurance, and creativity to be really evil. The big things—genocide, chairpersonship in a major corporation, murder—are beyond most folks. But that doesn't get us off the hook; there are plenty of "little" evils that we are all more than capable of.

Let's take just one example: evil speech or language. In the four Gospels the word *evil* can be found something like forty-one times, and half the time—*half*—it has to do with speech. To re-state the old children's adage, "Sticks and stones may break bones, but words will drop the hammer on your punk behind." When we talk, to rip off an old commercial, evil happens.

The reality, of course, is that there is evil in the world—both the big and the little kind. And we will want to stand up against evil, however we find it—in the big places and the little. We'll want to do what's right, maybe even no matter the cost. But we need to be careful; after all, when we start standing up against the evils others are practicing, even with the best of intentions, there is the danger that we will fall right into evil of our own.

So what can we do about the problem of evil? We can ask God to "set a guard over our mouths" (Psalm 141:3) so that we do not "sin with our tongue" (Psalm 39:1). We can remember that it is precisely while we are sinners that God loves us (Romans 5:8). And we can do those things for one another. Trust God and love your neighbor; that's the about best solution to evil you could find.

See also: fall, the; sin; older siblings

excommunication \ehks-kuh-myoo-nih-кĀ-shuhn\ n.

The act by which a community performs addition by subtraction.

Not to be confused with a loathe-letter sent to a former spouse, *excommunication* is the separation of a person from God's community. Typically a sinner (or one who is seen as a troublemaker) is removed from good standing in a church. The need for excommunication is difficult to understand, since the person is excluded

E

from the very thing that every sinner needs—God, God's grace, and God's people. But in extreme cases when a person is destroying a community or is a threat to others, it may be necessary. Often excommunication is self-imposed—either a person who thinks herself unworthy of God's love tragically leaves the community, or a person who thinks himself better than everyone else bails out on God's grace.

E

See also: church; simultaneously saint and sinner

existentialism \eh-ksih-STEHN-shuh-lih-zuhm\ n.

A philosophical telescope that zooms in extra close on human experience and identity, which often leads practitioners to engage in existence-threatening vices such as smoking, drinking, and the like.

Jean Paul Sartre, twentieth-century poster boy for existentialist philosophy, famously asserted, "Hell is other people!" We're quite sure he was a hoot at parties. Fascinated by the nonscientific, irreducible aspects of being human, existentialists wrote about boredom, despair, angst, lust, and dread. Christian existentialism explores the murky waters of the individual's experience of God, FAITH, and doubt. Much existentialist thought has some roots in the work of two nineteenth-century figures: Danish Lutheran Søren Kierkegaard and German Lutheran-gone-over-to-the-dark-side Friedrich Nietzsche.

See also: experience

experience \ehk-SPEER-ee-ihnts\ n., v.

The third cousin not-quite-far-enough-removed of having a clue, experience is something the Christian can't live without but can't quite live with, either.

Experience is one of those things that if you have it you don't need it, and if you need it you probably don't have it . . . and if you think you want to get it, you are in need of it in a way that precludes your ever getting enough of it.

Let's begin again. Experience is the personal encounter with God and faith. Thus, experience is both something that you cannot have Christian faith without . . . and at the same something that is dangerous and can threaten Christian faith.

On the one hand, you can't have faith without experience. You learn to pray by praying, to obey by obeying, to follow by following, and so on. You get to know what it is like to live as a forgiven person by learning to recognize your sins, feel sorry for them, and hear those sweet words, "In the name of Jesus Christ, your sins are forgiven." You get to know that God is guiding your life by looking back in time and recognizing, "Hey, when I was going through that junky time, God was there helping me!"

On the other hand, experience can be dangerous to faith. Why? Because sometimes it feels like God isn't there. Sometimes it feels like God is not listening to our prayers. Sometimes it feels like our sins are so big that they can't be forgiven. Sometimes it feels like either God has abandoned us or that maybe there isn't a God.

So, don't trust your experience; trust God, who has promised to be there for you.

See also: faith; forgiveness; prayer

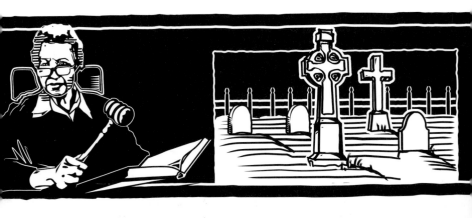

F

faith \fāth\ n.

Either a mustard seed, or a mountain-moving maelstrom, or a bit of both, if you're into mixed metaphors.

Faith is one of those funny ideas. We talk about having it, but we can't hold it or see it or touch it. We talk about strengthening it, but we can't do reps or test its limits against our progress.

Wouldn't it be nice if you could produce and improve faith in the same way that scientific research produces and improves just about everything else? You know, ask a question, develop a hypothesis, draft a procedure, conduct experiments, arrive at conclusions. This method works well for General Electric, but not so well with Jesus—which is good, because who wants a Jesus with a limited ninety-day warranty?

Faith is about the stuff in life that you can't measure with a dip-stick, test with a thermometer, or see through a microscope. Why? Because faith is about God, eternal life, forgiveness, grace, and all of that good stuff. Faith is about who you are and who God is. And can you measure who you are by using a dipstick (whether or not you *are* a dipstick)? Or, for that matter, can you measure who you are by measuring your grades, paychecks, or taxable square footage?

This isn't unique to us modern-day faith-seekers. Back in Bible times the disciples asked Jesus to "increase" their faith (Luke 17:5–6). So Jesus basically said, "If you had even a little faith, you could command a tree to jump in a lake, and it would do it for you." Jesus wasn't exactly serious, he was just messin' with them a little so that they would understand something about faith. The point isn't how much faith you have but who your faith is in. Trust Jesus, even a little bit, and you've got it!

If we put our trust in anything or anybody else, like an elected offi-cial, our pastor, or ourselves, that's what we like to call that age-old problem of idolatry. It was a bad idea when Aaron offered his revel-ing up to the golden calf (Exodus 32) and when Judas put his trust in a length of hemp, and it's still a very bad idea.

A word of caution: no matter how strong our faith is, God will always remain a mystery to human minds. God is greater than any idea of God we can whip up. But that doesn't mean we throw our hands up in the air and stop thinking; thinking is part of faith. Faith includes knowledge—knowing who God is, what God teaches, and what God promises. You can't just use your heart; you have to use your head.

Faith includes asking questions and trying on different answers. And faith includes following Jesus—following where Jesus leads, following his example, following his law, and obeying his commandments.

In the end, faith is the way we receive God. God has chosen to work through promises. God makes promises to us. And the only way to receive a promise is to have faith in the person who makes it.

See also: Christ (Messiah); disciple; free will; Jesus; Word of God

F

faithfulness \FĀTH-fuhl-nihss\ n.

God's way of being in our lives without living our lives for us.

Have you ever heard someone say, "God can do whatever God wants because God is God." An interesting idea. If you think God is a bully, that is.

Maybe God can do whatever God wants. But here's the deal. God has promised to do certain things and not to do certain other things. In other words, God has promised that God won't do whatever God wants. God has promised that even though God may at times want to do (or not do) some things, God won't do them (or will do them).

God won't . . . abandon you, disown you, drown the world in a flood, refuse to forgive your sins when you repent, live your life for you or turn you into a puppet, and so on.

God will . . . love you, forgive you, bless you, be with you, stick with you and the entire world to the very end.

Because God is faithful.

See also: free will; sovereignty

fall, the \thuh-fahl\ n.

Why—in our heart of hearts—we each believe we could out-god God.

Have you been wondering why you can't seem to get anything right—why you do things that you don't really want to, or don't do things that you wish you would? (How are those resolutions you copy-and-pasted from last year treating you this year?) We've been wondering the same thing about you. And lucky for you, we know the truth: you're a garden-variety fallen sinner. Before you start feeling too bad about yourself, here's the whole truth: so are we. So is everybody. Sucks to be us, doesn't it?

There's this story in Genesis where Adam and Eve disobeyed God's direct order not to eat fruit from this one particular tree. Ever told a kid not to touch something? Yeah, that's basically how it went down. A snake taunted them, and they went for it. The snake said, "Eat it and you'll be like God, knowing right from wrong." Once they ate the fruit, they could tell right from wrong. But funny thing— the ability to *know* right from wrong didn't give us the ability to *choose* right over wrong.

So not only had they rebelled against God, they made themselves a little more like God. Basically, that was the end. Or at least, the end of the beginning.

This incident, which describes humanity's broken condition, is sometimes known as (cue soundtrack: *dum dum dum*) . . . "The Fall." Theologians like to capitalize otherwise normal words and put them in quotations.

"The Fall" drop kicked Adam, Eve, and all humanity into quite the spiral: away from innocence and away from God.

We're not trying to sugar coat the screw-up when we point out that Adam and Eve don't really "fall down" but "rebel up." They wanted to "be like God" and not stay in their place—even though the place was paradise! So "The Downward Fall" is really (*dum dum dum*) "The Upward Rebellion." People were not satisfied to be creatures; they wanted to be like God.

The whole point of the story, of course, is that it describes accurately who we are. We want to be in charge, especially when we're not. We can't resist doing dumb stuff. We are broken, finite, limited, bound-to-screw-it-up people. And even when we try to do the right thing, sometimes it doesn't come out the way we intended. (Sort of like when Coca-Cola tried the "New Coke" back in the 1980s—boy was that screw-up.)

The story of "The Fall" tells the truth about us, our natures, and the brokenness of all creation. And the truth is, it can suck to be us.

Hold tight. We swear it's going to get better. Probably.

Dwell on humanity's collective jerkdom for just another second. Ever wanted to be good, but couldn't? Wanted to stop doing bad, but didn't? Wanted to tell the truth, but ended up lying? You, friend, are a product of "The Fall." Humans act like we are all the god that we need. We like to make ourselves happy at others' expense. If it's bad, we probably want it. If you tell us it's bad, then we want it for sure, and want it twice. No matter what we do or say, no matter how carefully we live, we are completely and totally unable to redeem ourselves from the hell of our own making.

But here's where the story *actually* gets better: the story is not the end of the story. Thanks to the death and resurrection of Jesus Christ, humanity's got a second shot. His one-time action opens the door to undoing the condition into which we are all born and, through grace by faith, making us into new creations. There is hope. Thank God.

See also: anthropology; Christ (Messiah); resurrection; sin

forgiveness \fur-GIHV-nihs\ n.

An act or quality we expect in our neighbor and God but practice ourselves only reluctantly.

When it comes to forgiveness, we believe it's time for a little truth-telling. There's lots of talk about forgiveness—how to do it, why it's important for a healthy relationship or a healthy society, how it's just as good for the forgiver as it is for the forgive-ee. All of this is probably true. But it's not the whole truth. So here's what we've got for you: a little "says/means." We'll give you what people say (something maybe you've said) and then tell you what people really mean by it.

Here's what you'll hear some people *say*: "I'll forgive you for what you did, but I can't forget it." Here's what they really *mean*: "Okay, I'm not ready to press charges in this relationship, but I'm going to put this one in the YBJ file ('You're a Big Jerk'). And when the time is right, I *will* bring it up again, and my case against you will be crushing."

F

The problem with this is that it isn't forgiveness. This forgive-but-not-forget thing is to real forgiveness as instant coffee is to a triple-shot latte. To forgive-but-not-forget is to say, "I accept your apology, now accept this lovely parting gift, a kick in your behind."

Or how about this. *Say*: "Forgiveness is really not for *them*, it's for *you*—you'll be happier and healthier if you just let it go." *Mean*: "They're not worth it, and you're better than them. So own your own anger, realize that they are not worth loving, and let it go."

This isn't forgiveness either. It isn't loving someone and therefore letting go of some wrong done to you; this is grudge-holding, letting go of the someone who wronged you and loving yourself.

Last one. *Say*: "There is no revenge so complete as forgiveness (Josh Billings). Always forgive your enemies—nothing annoys them so much (Oscar Wilde)." *Mean*: "If you really want to stick it to them, do the opposite of what they deserve." This kind of thinking is actually based on a biblical bit of wisdom, a truism about repaying your enemies with good things (Proverbs 25:21–22). But this isn't exactly forgiveness; it's more like strategies for sticking it to them.

So what *is* forgiveness? Forgiveness is complete and final. Forgiveness is what God does for us when Jesus shed his blood (Matthews 26:28). What's more, forgiveness is what's expected of people who are in relationship with God. Here's a quote that we actually like: "To err is human; to forgive divine" (Alexander Pope). In other words, we are at our most divine and closest to God when we forgive. God is the forgiver, the one who forgives us and makes it possible for us to forgive each other. And because all of us are sinners, forgiveness is an ongoing thing—we need it often, and we need to do it often. Just like Jesus said (Matthew 18:21).

See also: absolution; grace; judgment; love; mercy

free will \free-wihl\ n.

The belief—which you have no choice but to believe—that human beings are free to make their own choices.

So you think you have free will? Then try choosing not to believe in free will. Your heart and breathing will stop, and you will choke on your own spit before you can stop believing in free will. Or turn to the entry on PREDESTINATION right now. If you're not sure whether you have free will, then you may freely choose to keep reading this entry on free will. Hey, look at that. You're still reading. Was your choice to keep reading really free? Or was your choice to keep reading simply *bound* to what you already wanted to do?

The above paragraph is an example of the sort of brain teaser that inevitably results from discussions about free will.

In fact, God gives us *partial* free will. There are some things that God allows us to choose: what we eat for breakfast, the color of our hair (with chemical enhancement), and those sorts of things. And there are some things that God says, "This matter is too difficult for you, so I'll make your choice of you." Like whether or not God will have a relationship with you. God says, "I *will* have a relationship with you. I have already chosen you because I love you. Even if you *will* not to love me back." The *will* will *will* what it *will*, after all. But if you still think you have a free will in all things, check out the entry on PREDESTINATION.

See also: election; gospel; grace

glory \GLOHR-ee\ n.

An indefinable fine quality that is used to describe the indescribable.

God is glorious. Duh—and the sun is hot. There is no glory like that of the Almighty. Yeah, and water is wet. Where does this get us?

Glory is just one of those things that can be hard to wrap your brain around, maybe because it's a two-bit (for those of you under eighty that means "little") word trying to say something about God. Little words have a hard time doing that,

94

words like . . . GRACE . . . LOVE . . . MERCY . . . CROSS . . . RIGHTEOUS . . .
FORGIVENESS . . . friend . . . oh, that is glory—all of it together. We'll
just pipe down now.

See also: omni-[fill in the blank]; praise

God \gahd\ n.

The One who is completely other and absolute yet absolutely concerned with little ol' you.

G

Allow us to introduce Duh to you. The thing about Duh is that Duh
just doesn't get it. No matter how you explain it or how clearly you
paint the picture, Duh just doesn't get it. You probably know people
like Duh. Truth is, all of us have at least a little Duh in us.

Much of what you've heard about God is true. Creator of all things?
Check. Savior of the world? Double-check. Being with absolute wisdom and strength? Also true. But people also tend to have some
pretty strange ideas about God. Duh tends to have lots of conversa-
tions with God, so maybe Duh can help sort this one out. (You'll
meet Duh again in the GRACE article.)

Duh: So, God, who are you? What's your name?

God: *I am who I am. It's funny, Moses asked me that exact same
      question once. I gave him the same answer in Exodus 3:14. I
      don't think he liked the answer then, either, but at least you're
      in good company.*

Duh: What kind of name is that? I want a God I can talk to, take a closer walk with, relate to, and ask for stuff. I want a God who will be my big spiritual ATM and give me what I want.

God: *Isn't it enough that I know your name? And as for relating to me, on some level you just have to understand that you and I are on really, really different levels. I can relate to you, but you'll never be able to relate to me, since I am immortal, invisible, God only wise—because I am, you know, who I am.*

Duh: But there is a part of me that wants desperately to know you. There is a part of me that just won't ever be at peace unless I know you. I will be restless until I find my rest in thee . . . wait a minute, God, I think I feel a poem coming on.

God: *Oh my Me. Duh, I don't think the world could stand a poem by you.*

Duh: But I need to know you.

God: *I know. In fact, I made you that way. That's why I came down to earth in the flesh and blood of Jesus Christ—in him I speak your language. That is why I make myself known to you in ways you can get, why I chose Israel and blessed them to be my blessing for the rest of the world. That is why I sent prophets and teachers and gave you the Bible.*

Duh: But I still have questions. Do you know everything? See everything? Have total power? If you are good, why do bad things happen? Why did Jesus have to die? How can you be One God and three persons? How can you be both seated in heaven and everywhere on earth? What happens after death? What happened to my G.I. Joe when I lost him in second grade?

God: *Great questions, Duh. For right now, focus on one thing. First, if you want to know me, get to know Jesus. You can't see me, but I put on human flesh so that you could know me. So get to know Jesus.*

G

See also: Well . . . all the other articles.

gospel \GAH-spuhl\ n.

The message about Jesus's death and resurrection, which is always good and always new, and thus most people are bored by it.

There was this street preacher hanging out on the corner, getting his scream on about how the world had already reached medium-well-done and was about to be completely overcooked in a fiery ending. People on the sidewalk avoided him by walking in the street. The *street people* avoided him by sleeping in the street. And the preacher ended his jalapeño-induced rant by declaring, "This is the *gospel* of Jesus Christ!"

Back off there, Betty Crocker! You tell people that the world is going to get deep fried like a New Orleans beignet, and you say this is the *gospel?*

A little basic Bible learning might help here. The word *gospel* actually means "good news." It comes from the Greek word *euangelion*, which in turn is a compound word made of the Greek parts *eu* (meaning "good," as in euphemism, a nice way of saying something unpleasant) and *angelia* (meaning "message," as in, well, a message). Our English terms EVANGELICAL and EVANGELISM are related to this word.

G

The gospel message is good news. More specifically, it is a particular sort of good news—the news that Jesus Christ was crucified, died, and raised for you. And this is a good thing, which is why even though the scare tactics employed by certain testosterone-juiced hell-and-damnation preachers may sometimes be effective (after all, Jesus died to forgive our sins), they are inappropriate.

So what is the good news? Two different Bible passages summarize the good news. Memorize these, and you'll never regret it:

1. "For God so loved the world that he gave his only Son, so that everyone who believes in him may not perish but may have eternal life" (John 3:16).

2. "In Christ God was reconciling the world to himself, not counting their trespasses against them, and entrusting the message of reconciliation to us" (2 Corinthians 5:19).

The gospel is both a particular message and a particular way of delivering a message.

About the message: the basic message of the gospel is that *God has acted decisively and permanently in Jesus.* The gospel isn't something that tells us that we have to do something; it tells us what God has done for us. People are always trying to mess with the gospel by adding conditions to it. They like to say stuff like, "God helps those who help themselves." This messing-with-the-gospel garbage turns us into the ones who do stuff (for example, "help ourselves"). The gospel is good news because God is the one who acts.

About the way of delivering the message: because the gospel is "good news," it can only be delivered in ways that the audience will hear it as good news. In the history of the church, sometimes sadly misled Christians baptized or converted people by force. Or during the civil rights conflict in America, so-called Christians burned crosses as messages of hate. This is not the gospel. The good news requires speech and behavior that leads to the message of Jesus being heard as good news.

See also: atonement; evangelical; judgment; salvation

grace \grās\ n. (but more like a v.)

The free gift in which God gives everything—eternal life, forgiveness, purpose, meaning—to human beings, who respond by trying to earn it.

One time God was trying to explain grace to Duh.

Duh: "God, the Bible says that we are 'justified by your grace as a gift' (Romans 3:24). Since I want to be justified, how do I get this grace?"

God: *Well, Duh, grace is not something that I give you so that you can be saved, it is the way that I save you. Grace is the way that I accept you, the way that I love you. Grace means that I love you not because of anything you do but just because I love you. Grace means that I save you from death and give you eternal life as a free gift—you don't have to do anything in order to be saved.*

Duh: Okay. I get that I don't have to do something to have a relationship with you. But what if I have done something really bad—like committed murder or adultery, or burned down my neighbor's house just because? What if I have broken every one of the Ten Commandments many times?

God: *Same thing. Grace means that I love you even if you have done something really bad. Grace means that there is nobody who has done anything so that I don't still love them. Grace means that even adulterers and murderers are my children.*

Duh: So I don't have to do anything to be saved, and there is nothing I can to stop you from saving me. But what about after I am saved? Don't I have to quit sinning?

God: *Duh, I know you pretty well. I know that after I save you, you'll try to change. But I know that until you die, you'll still be a sinner who sins. I love sinners—I sent my Son to die for sinners, for heaven's sake! Grace means that there is nothing you can do to make me stop loving you.*

Duh: But what about REPENTANCE and FAITH—don't I have to repent and have faith?

God: *Faith and repentance are things that* you *do. Faith is the way you receive a promise. My grace is a promise: the promise of eternal life, FORGIVENESS, and a relationship with me. The only way to receive a PROMISE is to believe it. Repentance is similar; it is what happens to you when my word reaches you, and you realize that you need me. So faith and repentance aren't things that you do. My word creates them.*

G

Duh: So you are saying I don't have to do anything.

God: *Duh!*

See also: justification; means of grace; works, good

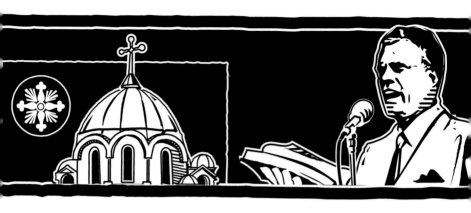

• • • • **H** • • • •

happy exchange \HA-pee-ehks-CHĀNJ\ n.

Unlike your spouse, who says "everything that is yours is mine and everything that is mine is mine," this comes from a fancy-schmancy Latin term (see *communicatio idiomatum* below) in which God says, "Everything that is mine is yours, and everything that is yours is mine."

Does $100,000 sound good? Maybe at first, but not when you know that this is how much the Boston Red Sox received when they sold Babe Ruth to the New York Yankees. Most baseball aficionados (a fancy term for "nerds") consider this the worst (or best) swap in the history of baseball.

The swap that God made when Jesus died for us appears to be another lopsided trade. When God became human in Jesus Christ,

God agreed "to bear the sins of many" (Hebrews 9:18). Christ makes a swap. He takes our imperfection, sin, guilt, death, and general suckiness. We get Christ's perfection, RIGHTEOUSNESS, innocence, and eternal life. Such a deal! It's no wonder that Luther called this the *fröhliche Wechsel* (if you say that out loud in an airport security line, you may get searched)—the "joyful exchange." What a deal!

This "communication of property" (*communicatio idiomatum*) happens when we are "clothed with Christ" in baptism. Through faith, we gain all of Christ's benefits. At the same time he takes our heaviest burdens upon himself. But don't think Jesus comes out on the short end of the stick. He gladly makes this trade with us because (a) he loves us, and (b) he gets to keep us forever. Again, what a deal.

See also: atonement; attributes of God; means of grace; sin

heaven \HEH-vuhn\ n.

The full reconciliation with God and the entire created order ... even with those parts we don't particularly like.

Heaven's not an eternal nap, nor a one-way ticket via Divine Airlines back to the garden of Eden, nor an everlasting round of golf (as some of those golf jokes would have you believe). Heaven means full reconciliation with God! What such an existence will be like, "no eye has seen and no ear has heard ... what God has prepared for those who love him" (as the apostle Paul put it). Still, don't be fooled by some versions of heaven that say we will become God ourselves. Know this: our reconciliation with God is very different from us becoming God. And know this: we will always be creatures, and that's a really good thing.

The Bible pictures heaven in a number of different ways. For instance, as a new Jerusalem coming down from heaven, as a marriage feast, as a choir of voices in all languages, as a party for the lost who have been found, and so on. Heaven will not be individuals pursuing eternal pleasure in isolation, like those lonely angels sitting on lonely clouds playing lonely harp tunes. Eternal life is a grand gathering of saints—we'll not only be reconciled with God but with each other. Heaven will not be Saint Peter's lonely harps club but a band of banjos!

What about all those people we don't like? Will they be in heaven too? Well, we'll leave that up to Jesus, who (unlike you) will judge the living and the dead. Rest assured, heaven will mean a new existence lived solely under God's boundless love; in this new existence there'll be joy and maybe even a little tolerance and acceptance.

See also: hell; judgment; salvation

hell \hehl\ or \HĀ-ehl\ n.

The place of complete separation from God; most people think they'll never go there but also think they know who will.

If someone says to you "Don't go there" when you bring up the subject of hell, you should probably take it as sound advice. In the New Testament hell is pictured as a place where there will be much gnashing of teeth—and where there will be no dental plan or health care of any kind. And there's a lake of fire but no indication of what lakeshore property is going for. The real point is that hell is that place where there is no relationship with God. In any case, you can trust Jesus to steer you toward much better real estate. As in all real estate, remember: location, location, location!

See also: death; heaven; judgment; Satan

heresy \hehr-uh-see\ n.

The official teaching that there are unofficial teachings that are officially contrary to the official teachings of the Christian faith; most of what you read in this book (just kidding).

Have you ever noticed that when someone tells you they "agree to disagree," they usually just can't accept that you're right and they're wrong? Yeah, us too. But then, we're always right, so we wouldn't know wrong if it slapped us in the face. Theologians are pretty smart. (And humble, too.)

For the sake of argument, let's say maybe at some point people did agree to disagree when it came to theology. The thing is, a disagreement about theology doesn't just mean you won't bring the subject up at dinner parties—it might actually be a matter of salvation. For this reason, the church has generally tried to get clear on what it agrees on, and it generally doesn't want people to disagree on some of those big points.

A *heresy*, at heart, started as a disagreement or an alternate concept but took a pretty dangerous turn and steered straight off the map. Think of Christian theology as a ginormous map, with dark border-lines near the edges. Within those lines, there is lots and lots of room to explore—huge tracks of land, tall mountains, deep oceans, and scenic historic sites. But beyond those boundaries? As the old maps used to say: *Here dragonnes dwelle.*

There are not that many official heresies, so don't start to think that Christianity is primarily a list of rules to believe about God. That's not really Christian faith. But there are some dragonne-dwelleing-area false teachings about following and believing in Jesus that are good to know.

Every Christian seeks to follow Jesus and believe in him. But there are ways of teaching about Jesus that don't teach the real Jesus and ways of following him that really have you following someone else. By the time the Christian church was almost 150 years old, there were enough of these false ways around to inspire a French guy (named Irenaeus) to write against these false ways in a book called, uh, *Against the Heresies.*

The catalogue of early Christian heresies (sects) reads like a grocery list of unpronounceable -isms. Here are some of the major -isms on which the early church agreed to disagree:

Valentinianism: Also called Gnosticism, the teaching that the world was an abortive creation by a lesser god and the way to salvation is through a handing down of secret knowledge. (The Greek fancy-pants term being *gnōsis*).

Marcionism: The teaching popularized by Marcion, who thought that the Old Testament God was evil and separate from the New Testament God. Marcion proposed that Christians reject the OT and read only the Gospel of Luke and a heavily edited (of all OT references) version of Paul's letters.

Manichaeism: The pleasingly adaptable heresy that picked up gods as it went along and preached a smushing together of the truths of the religions it met. It rejected the idea of an omnipotent [see omnipotence], loving God and taught that there is light and dark in all life.

Montanism: The teaching of a guy who claimed to be the Holy Spirit incarnate and spoke in tongues a lot so no one could argue with him.

Donatism: After a time of intense persecution, during which many Christians denied the faith, this teaching argued against letting those who had recanted on their faith back in to the church. Understandable, but it's a pesky thing, Christian forgiveness . . .

Arianism: A teaching that couldn't quite handle the Trinity but asserted that Jesus was created by the Father and thus possibly an inferior deity.

Pelagianism: The "chief heresy" of the faith—the teaching that Jesus's sacrifice didn't mean much since humans were in complete control of their actions and salvation and therefore responsible for every sin, error, and mistake they made. We bet these guys were a kick at parties.

Nestorianism: The teaching that Jesus had two separate essences, Jesus the human and Logos the divine, which existed together in one body.

And remember what the immortal Ferris Bueller said about -isms: "Isms in my opinion are not good. A person should not believe in an ism."

See also: Catholic; Christology; hypostatic union; orthodox; Protestant; Son of God; Trinity

history \HIH-stuh-ree\ n.

The onerous piling up and ordering of information—dates, names, events, places, people, and things—intended to illustrate moments of lasting importance, which usually results in their being rendered confusing.

Some modern academic smarty-trousers types might tell you, were you fool enough to ask them, that the ancient world (read: "olden days") had nothing like modern history writing. History, they'll

drone on in their Joe Friday worldview, is black and white—just the facts. The Bible, they'll likely add, is nothing of the sort. To them we say *phooey.*

There is probably a place for this view of history, but it doesn't fit Bible history. The Bible is not interested in "just the facts." Don't be offended, 'cause the people who wrote the Bible wouldn't be. The Bible is interested in *way more than the facts!* History in the Bible is written to make a point, inform hearts, and change minds. Just ask John about his Gospel and see what he says (like in 20:31). In the Bible, history is the story of salvation.

The Bible presents a picture of the history of God at work. So peoples' histories—like that of Israel or the church—are not so much histories of those people but histories of their understanding of God's work in, with, and for them. In other words, history is less about dates, names, events, places, people, and things, and more about a picture or description of God—in still other words, history is theology. Yes, we know, that is crazy talk.

See also: gospel; theology; tradition

holy \HOH-lee\ adj.

What you've been made, even if you don't know it or can't believe it.

holiness \HOH-lee-nihs\ n.

The state of being what you've been made.

We even hesitate to mention it since it usually just goes straight to people's heads, but we are all holy. After all, in the waters of baptism, God washes people clean. God grants holiness to all who have faith in the saving death and resurrection of Christ. Without doing anything, we've been claimed as God's own chosen children and promised eternal life.

If we're honest, we're also pretty big screw-ups. So how can we ever apply holiness to our crappy selves? The truth is, it's nothing that we've done that makes us holy—God alone can do that. Only God is holy in the sense of being pure, righteous, and perfect. But because of God's love and grace, we're each made holy. God "holifies" us, transferring God's quality of being holy to us.

Holiness, then, is not a lifestyle—it's a neighborhood. We live there because God bought the property and moved us in.

See also: grace; righteousness; simultaneously saint and sinner; sin

Holy Spirit \hoh-lee-SPEER-iht\ n.

The third person of the Trinity; sort of like Ringo, the Spirit is so active and vital that people either forget it's there or have an unhealthy fixation on it.

The Holy Spirit is the active presence of God in CREATION. It is the drumbeat that lays down the rhythm and provides the drive for the music, the dance, and the lyrics. Since it's also called the Holy Ghost, the Spirit often gets sidelined as being too strange, elusive, or creepy for regular conversation and use. Therefore, the Spirit is often forgotten by Christians or left for those weirdo believers who tend to put their hands in the air during worship or scream unintelligibly. But really, the Spirit is simply the active presence of God here and now and for all eternity, but apparently that's hard to grasp.

The Holy Spirit can be hard to understand and pin down because the Holy Spirit doesn't get as many headlines as the other two persons of the Trinity. While God the Father stars in creation and throughout the Old Testament and God the Son got the lead role in all four Gospels, God the Spirit is like the musical score of a movie—you don't notice it unless it's not there. It's time to get over our heebie-jeebies about a holy ghost thing with a sheet over her head and realize that the Spirit is well documented biblically and essential doctrinally. Brace yourselves.

Some theological-type people argue for the Spirit's presence in Genesis 1:2, where we hear reference to a spirit or the breath of God moving over the water. This is often seen as an expression of the Holy Spirit moving in creation. It is active today, as it was then, as

H

God's life-giving force on earth (very Star Trek, we know, but go with it). It was there at the beginning and is present in the world still. The Spirit is not just a pretty face—the Spirit has created and sustains creation.

Later on we read that the Holy Spirit made it so Jesus could be born of Mary. In John 20:22, Jesus breathes this same Holy Spirit right back out onto the disciples, granting them the authority to forgive sins. The Spirit's biggest moment came in Acts 2 at the first Pentecost, when it came like fire and gave the disciples the power to speak in tongues and preach the good news about Jesus. So the Holy Spirit is also very much tied up in the presence of Jesus himself. In fact, Jesus refers to the Spirit as the power by which God keeps the church faithful and true. Finally, the Spirit is active creating gifts and fruits among God's people—such as LOVE, peace, patience, preaching, teaching, and FAITH. The Spirit sustains the witness and work of the church, just like it did at the first Pentecost.

Maybe the Holy Spirit isn't as well known as the other two persons, but there is no power more vital in creation. You're going to want a piece of that.

See also: Christ (Messiah); God; Jesus; Pentecost; spiritual gift; Trinity

hope \hohp\ n.

The promise of a future worth the trouble it takes to get out of bed in the morning.

Intimately related to faith and love (see 1 Corinthians 13) and quite unlike fear, dread, and sarcasm, hope is one of those things that we human beings cannot generate from within. Hope starts to grow inside of us when a promise is spoken to us from the outside. Theologically, this means hope is our response to the gospel, and it means hope has the same invigorating and optimism-producing properties as a great cup of coffee on a cold, dark morning. In contrast to strong java, however, the effects of gospel-induced hope are longer lasting (we are promised eternal life), free (we don't have to pay for hope, not even for fair-trade, organically grown hope), and of some benefit to one's NEIGHBOR (because we have hope, we also have love for the neighbor).

See also: eschatology; faith; love

hypostatic union \HI-puh-sta-tihk-YOO-nyuhn\ n.

The ultimate mystery as a math equation: JC=(DN)(HN)=1P, where JC stands for Jesus Christ, DN stands for Divine Nature, HN stands for Human Nature, and 1P stands for One Person.

Those crazy early Christian leaders were always fine-tuning their crazy talk. The church had already declared that Jesus was 100 percent God and 100 percent human. But *how* was Jesus both of these? It took about a century and a half, but in 451 CE, at a council in the ancient city of Chalcedon (part of present day Istanbul), they finally got it exactly, perfectly, hair-splittingly, crazy-talkingly right. The term *hypostatic union* means that the two natures of Jesus are united in one person (that is, in one "essence"). *Hypostasis* is a term straight out of Greek philosophy. Literally, *hypostasis* means "that which lies underneath, as with a foundation." In other words, you can't say

that Jesus's body was human and that his spirit was divine—rather, divine and human were both united in his one essence.

See also: Christ (Messiah); Christology; doctrine; heresy; incarnation; Jesus; Trinity

idol \ɪ-duhl\ n.

That thing you think is serving you but is really enslaving you.

So you think you only worship one god? Well, imagine "being you" without your career, money, good health, success, alcohol, or favorite band—"more cowbell" anyone? An idol is anything other than God that we love or put our trust in. In Bible days, people worshiped gods of fertility, gods of war, a golden calf, human beings such as pharaoh or caesar, and so on. Today? Money, sex, sports, self-esteem, trophy spouses, political ideologies—any of those little things about you that you think make you better than "those people." We imagine we control these things, but often it is the opposite. But the true God shows power in this way: when those things let us down, God is there in the depths of our lows—never abandoning us, saving us from false gods.

See also: God; worship

image of God \IH-mihj-uhv-GAHD\ n.

The un-credible teaching that human beings are in some way like God; a teaching made more un-credible when one gets a good look at one's neighbor and still more un-credible when one looks in the mirror. (If you're into snooty Latin crazy talk, we call this the *imago Dei*.)

If you were to take the concept that every human being is created in the image of God to its logical conclusion, then you would either have to allow that God could appear as nothing more than an extremely well-developed chimp or entertain the possibility that God might look something like your Uncle Stanley—comb-over, lazy eye, beer belly, the whole nine yards. (Maybe that also describes your Aunt Flo.)

That all sounds just a little cynical doesn't it? Well, that's part of our point.

We have a tendency to look at one another—or when we're feeling really blue or bad or down, even at ourselves—and see the worst. Looking at one another, we do not see a reflection of God but an image of the half-evolved, lesser side of our nature—sloping foreheads, dragging knuckles, backward senses of fashion. And that's a big part of our problem when it comes to living together.

Do you remember what God thought after making everything? God saw that "it was good." That bit's in Genesis 1:4 . . . and verses 10, 12, 18, 21, and 25, too. God saw lots of the stuff that God had made and saw that it was good. And would you expect anything else? It is God doing the making after all. But none of this was "in the image" of God. It was all made *by* God, according to God's *design*, with an image in God's eye; but this was not the *image of God*. Only when God makes people—both male and female—does God's image come into play. God makes us—yes, you and your neighbors next door and down the road and around the world—in this same image, namely, God's image. And from God's point of view we—yes, you too, and all the rest—look pretty darn good, even if we're not perfect.

This is good news for all of us and wonderful news for you. You bear the image of God. You are something special, no matter what you may be tempted to think about yourself. And here's the good news for you neighbor—she bears the image of God too, and that's something that we should and can try to see a little more of in one another. We humans bear God's image, and we can bear God's point of view as well—we can see that good, worthy, and wonderful things are all around us.

See also: creation; Son of God

immanence of God \IH-muh-nuhnts-uhv-GAHD\ n. + prep. + pr. n.

The glasses on your face, the rings in your ear, what you search for even though you have it already.

Ever look for your glasses for ten minutes, only to realize that they were on your head the whole time? Or look for your keys but they were in your hand? God's immanence—meaning "within" or "nearness"—says that God is like that. Even as you search for God, God is already near. "For what other great nation has a god so near as the Lord our God is whenever we call to him?" (Deuteronomy 4:7).

See also: transcendence of God

incarnation \ihn-kar-NĀ-shuhn\ n.

The out-of-this-world notion that the eternal and infinite God came down to this earth in the finite and first-century Jesus of Nazareth.

If you've ever been to Texas (or a decent supermarket) . . . sorry, if y'all've ever been to Texas . . . you've probably tasted chili. And if you've ever made yourself up a good vat of chili, you know that the ingredients are simple: some nice hot chilis, some great tomato sauce, some cumin, and some good beans. But wait, something is missing . . . the meat! (Sorry vegans, this joke isn't for you—it only works with meat.) For an out-of-this-galaxy taste adventure, you have to have meat. This type of chili is, of course, chili *con carne* (with meat). And this relates to Jesus because . . .

. . . you can't get a decent grasp on who Jesus is if you don't grasp that Jesus is God incarnate, or to put it in the terms of our chili chef, God *in carne* (in the flesh). Sure, Jesus is one part great theological teacher, one part social revolutionary, one part miracle worker, one part great moral hero, and at least a half cup of a truly great spiritual role model. But to really understand Jesus, you need to know that he is God-with-us.

On the one hand, Jesus is exactly like one of us. On the other hand, Jesus so completely surpasses any of us. Both of these statements are true. Jesus is both human (like us) and divine (way surpassing us). But before we start dissecting Jesus and labeling his big toe human and his heart divine, we need to get one thing straight. Jesus isn't half God and half human; he's *fully* God and *fully* human. Just let the math go.

We might not ever think about it, but in the Apostles' Creed, we confess Christ's incarnation. "He was conceived by the power of the Holy Spirit and born of the Virgin Mary." That he was conceived by the power of the Spirit means that he was *fully God* in the flesh. He came to earth on a mission unlike any other (to save the world), with power and possibilities unlike any other, and he even shared the mind of God.

But that he was born of the Virgin Mary means that he was fully God *in the flesh*. It's easy to forget, but Jesus came into the world the same way we all do—the birth canal. His presence wasn't spiritual, but he was real flesh and blood. Heresy alert! In the early church (and still today), a teaching emerged that downplayed the human elements of Jesus's life and uplifted his deity. The early church saw the danger in this teaching. If we deny the humanity of Jesus, we deny the good news that makes us Christian.

So let's delve into his humanity. He had to be fed, potty trained (wonder what his chair looked like), and taught. That'll throw you, won't it? He wasn't just God *pretending* to be a human; he was completely human in every aspect of his life.

See also: Christ (Messiah); Christology; heresy; hypostatic union; Jesus

inclusive language \ihn-ᴋʟoo-sihv-ʟāɴ-gwihj\ n.

The arrangement of the grammatical furniture in such a way that no one sits comfortably.

Ever since Moses asked God, "Um . . . who can I say is calling?" and got some confusing word play in reply (see Exodus 3 for the whole story), a whole pile of languages, images, and metaphors have been put into the service of getting a comfy picture of God. Describing God by way of analogy to human beings has been popular, effective, and troublesome since day one. Inclusive language proponents note that most Christians throughout history have been running on the assumption that God bats for the boy team—that is, we tend to refer to God as a "he." They want more linguistic options and point out that exclusive use of male metaphors for God seems to run counter to the biblical teaching that both male *and* female human beings were created in the ɪᴍᴀɢᴇ ᴏꜰ ɢᴏᴅ (see Genesis 1:26–27). The point is this: God is not a human male. Or female.

The inclusive language debate shows us a tricky thing with all this crazy God talk—the ongoing human tendency to imagine a god created in our image rather than worship God. We tend to take what we like best about ourselves—everything from strong muscles to a sweet disposition to vegetarianism to our gender-specific plumbing. This goes for the folks on both sides of the inclusive language conversation, by the way.

God is not an amalgam of the best ideas we can come up with but a free and distinct being with a personality, a plan, and a passion to be in relationship with all of us. What is inclusive about God is God's love for the entire scope of creation and God's desire and intention to reach and redeem everything. When we describe God in terms—or pronouns—that drive some people away from God, we fail both God and each other.

See also: attributes of God; God; idol; ontology; worship; YHWH

indulgence \in-DUHL-juhnts\ n.

A dreamy confection that left such a bad taste that it started a reformation.

To *indulge* means to be generous or lenient to the point of excess. In churchy talk, an *indulgence* was meant to be something generous and lenient. But instead, *indulgences* became burdensome and oner-ous. The history of how indulgences became a thing in Christianity is fascinating. So what are you waiting for? Google it—we'll wait.

You're back. Great. See? Isn't that fascinating? We told you it would be. So you can imagine why people objected when the church adver-tised that you and your loved ones could get to heaven faster just by making a donation to the church building fund. One sixteenth-cen-tury advertisement put it this way: "As soon as your money is given, another soul will get to heaven!" Um. No. In the end, it's better just to indulge in a bowl of ice cream. And leave the getting to heaven in God's hands.

See also: forgiveness; justification; Reformation

inerrancy \ihn-EHR-uhn-tsee\ n.

The idea that something that is not God is perfect—as only God is.

If you've ever played cards, you may be familiar with "trump"—not Donald, but hearts, spades, diamonds, and clubs. In theology the ultimate trump card is the idea of inerrancy—the claim that some-thing is without error. Different people try to play trump cards by claiming the papal office, the Bible, the Koran, science, reason, the free market, and so on are without error. But life ain't cards. And only God is perfect. Besides, even if, say, the Bible were inerrant, imperfect humans are still the ones understanding and applying it to life. Life is a no-trump game.

See also: Bible; interpretation; revelation

interpretation \ihn-tuhr-prih-TĀ-shuhn\ n.

The act of bending one's tiny and inflexible mind around something big and three-dimensional—such as Scripture, life, or God.

Anytime anyone interacts with information, they have to interpret it. That means that whether you like it or not, you're a biblical interpreter. Welcome to an incredibly boring job that you didn't even know you had and won't get you any money unless, like us, you decide to write a witty book about it.

If you've ever read a book, watched a movie, talked with a friend, or tried to understand your spouse's body language, you have engaged in interpretation. Human life requires understanding. (Fancy-pants philosophers term this "hermeneutics" or "making meaning" and many other crazy things.) We can only do this by taking in, processing, and acting on the things we see, hear, and do in our lives. However, in the case of Scripture, we aren't just interpreting a book; we're interpreting the Word of God (insert big, echoing soundtrack).

In order for the Bible to make sense in our lives, it must be processed and digested like any other tasty bit of food. And no, that's not a literal statement—in spite of the fact that Ezekiel ate a scroll. We don't recommend eating your Bible, but we do recommend "chewing it over" (and over, and over, and over). In fact, the metaphor of "chewing the Bible over" comes from Psalm 1. There, the psalm writer says the "happy" or "blessed" person "meditates on" God's Word day and night. The word "meditate" in Hebrew can be translated more literally as "ruminate."

So how do you interpret the Bible? Well, it is an art, not a science. It takes lots of practice. It should be done in groups, not alone. It is a holy act, so begin with prayer. And here are a few other guidelines to keep in mind.

1. *Type of literature.* Interpret each part of Scripture for what it is. When you read a newspaper, you interpret a news story differently from an opinion article, which you interpret differently from a comic—but there is truth in each. Do the same with different parts of the Bible.

2. *Context.* Interpret a passage in its context. Leviticus 3:16 says, "All fat belongs to the Lord." You might think, *Cool, pass the chips*, but the context shows it is about burnt offerings.

3. *Don't pick just what you like.* You can't just pick the bits that support your opinion; this is called prooftexting, and it's a very naughty type of interpretation.

4. *The whole kaboodle.* You must take the work as a whole; this means no reading just the nice parts, which will turn God into a stuffed bunny.

5. *Openness.* Be open to an interpretation that clashes with your own preference. After all, that's when things get fun. And it just might be when you will hear God.

See also: Bible; inerrancy

Jesus \JEE-zuhs\ n.

Adopted son of a carpenter, born of a virgin girl, parable teller, miracle worker, crucified criminal, and the last person anyone would expect to save the entire world.

We talk about Jesus a lot—some of us without even realizing it. (His name tends to make a well-punctuated interjection.) Many people like to use his name, either in complete flippancy or total earnestness. But when the rubber hits the road—or, in JC's case, the feet hit the water's surface—these same people don't always know who they're talking about.

Before you think we're crazy—because clearly *everyone* knows exactly who Jesus is—let's settle a few questions: Was Jesus human or divine? Was he Joseph's son or God's son? A prophet, a teacher, a miracle worker, or a savior? A blessed savior or a cursed criminal? A powerless infant (Ricky Bobby likes this one the best) or an all-powerful judge?

If you're having trouble answering, you're in good company. The people Jesus met as he cruised all over Palestine and Jerusalem in his sandals couldn't figure out what to make of Jesus. The disciples asked, "Who then is this that even the winds and the sea obey him?" (Mark 4:41). The crowds wondered, "Is not this Joseph's son?" (Luke 4:22). When asked who he was, some people said, "John the Baptist . . . Elijah . . . or one of the prophets" (Mark 8:28). The Jew-

ish high priest asked, "Are you the Messiah, the Son of the Blessed One?" (Mark 14:61). The Roman governor asked, "Are you the King of the Jews?" (Mark 15:2).

Jesus himself said, "I am the bread of life" (John 6:35); "I am the light of the world" (John 8:12); "I am the gate/good shepherd" (John 10:7, 14); "I am the way, the truth, and the life" (John 14:6). Makes you wonder—was he having an identity crisis? Has there ever been someone about whom there were so many questions?

Thank God that the Holy Spirit helped Peter become the first one to figure it out: "You are the Messiah," he told Jesus (Mark 8:29). Ever since Peter confessed that truth, and ever since God raised Jesus from the dead, those who believe in Jesus have been trying to figure out what Jesus's identity as the Christ means for the rest of us. That is what faith is all about—trying to understand what Jesus means for us, and this takes an entire lifetime and then some.

And it takes a lot of books to explore what that means. To borrow a phrase from the Gospel of John, "If every one of them were written down, I suppose that the world itself could not contain the books that would be written" (21:25). Just think on this: Jesus is the fullest picture of what God is like that is available. If you know Jesus, you know God's love for you.

See also: Christ (Messiah); God; Holy Spirit; incarnation; Son of God; Trinity

J

judgment \JUHJ-mihnt\ n.

The justly deserved punishing and condemning action of God that one usually imagines will be directed toward one's neighbor rather than toward one's self.

One day, Duh was talking to God about judgment. (We assume you have already made Duh's acquaintance, but if not, see the entries on GOD and GRACE.) Duh, as you will remember, is one of those people who just has a hard time getting it. We all have at least a little bit of Duh in us.

Duh: Hey God. I've got some work here for you. I've been living in this neighborhood for a few years now and I've gotten to know my neighbors pretty well. And let me tell you, there is some smiting and punishing that needs to go down. We need some wailing and gnashing of teeth. So I've made a list of who's naughty, in no particular order. These folks deserve some fire and brimstone.

God: *Duh, I have one issue with your list: I don't seem to see your name on the list. You are a sinner, too, you know.*

Duh: Well, of course I know that I am a sinner, but I have been saved by grace through faith! And because I am saved, I kind of figured that I am like one of those cars with three or more people that gets to avoid the traffic lights in the on-ramp—that I am immune to judgment.

God: *[After a short pause . . . but remember a thousand ages in God's sight are like a moment gone.] Duh, who told you that you are immune to judgment?*

Duh: Well, you did, when you told me that there is nothing that I can do that will make you stop loving me or end our relationship.

God: *You don't have it quite right, Duh. Being saved means being forgiven; it does not mean immunity to judgment. Let me put it another way. To be forgiven is to be judged, and the verdict is, "You are guilty. And then you are forgiven, for Christ's sake." I never said that you aren't to be judged, only that when I look at you, I don't just see your sins, I also see my Son, Jesus, who gave his life for you.*

Duh: That's a little hard on my self-esteem, God. I'm not sure that my therapist will think too highly of your counseling.

Wouldn't it be more affirming of you just to accept rather than forgive me? Forgiveness seems to imply judgment, which is just so negative.

God: *You are almost getting it . . . but not quite. Forgiveness does indeed imply judgment, as I have already said. But this isn't negative; in fact, this is the best news that there is. You don't have to compare yourself to your neighbor. You don't have to lie to yourself about not being a broken person or pretend that you are immune to judgment. You just have to be honest about the fact that you are a broken, fallen person . . . and that you are forgiven and loved anyway. To be saved is to be judged and forgiven at the same time.*

See also: forgiveness; grace; law

J

justice \JUHS-this\ n.

A condition that most people desire for themselves, claim never to get, and have no interest in granting to their neighbors.

As we turn to a discussion of justice, we believe that complete and utter fair play is called for. Therefore, for the remainder of this article, we will refrain from irony, sarcasm, and other forms of humor. Furthermore, we will avoid both exaggeration and understatement. The passion in this article will arise solely from our sense of outrage at the inequity of which we have been victims.

Hear the outcry of one aggrieved: "I wanted a Big Wheel as a child and I never got one! But my little brother got a Big Wheel. It is time that the universe made up for this gross offense!"

(You didn't really believe that garbage about refraining from sarcasm, did you?)

Justice in the theological sense is about far more than being fair. As a police detective friend of ours says, "The fair is in August—it's where they judge pigs." It is not that fairness isn't important. It is. In fact, while we are generally against -isms, we count ourselves ardent adherents to the doctrines of "fairism." But theologically speaking, fairness is to justice as a Big Wheel is to a Harley Davidson. Justice is a far *bigger* concept.

Here is a concise definition: Justice is the ordering of society according to God's demands and in which all life can thrive. That is such a sweet definition, you should memorize it. Or tattoo it on your little brother, who got your Big Wheel.

Because justice is about God's preferred social order in which all life can thrive, it means that society must be more than merely fair. There must be special provision made for the disadvantaged. Don't take our word for it, take God's Word: "Learn to do good; seek justice, rescue the oppressed, defend the orphan, plead for the widow" (Isaiah 1:17). Once God was particularly angry with the chosen people and said this: "Hear this word, you cows of Bashan . . . who oppress the poor, who crush the needy." What did God want? "Let justice roll down like waters" (Amos 4:1; 5:24). (The cows of Bashan considered themselves better than the cows of Shittim, Assyria, and, above all, Dilmun.)

Maybe an example will help. The rules of sporting events are designed to be fair but not just. The rules exist so that the biggest, fastest, strongest, smartest, hardest working, and most well-prepared will win . . . and so that everyone else will lose. As long as we are talking about sports, fairness is good enough.

But God wants society to operate so that as many win as possible. It is okay if the big, strong, fast, smart, hardworking, and best-prepared win in the game of life. But God wants as many of the rest of us as possible to win in life too. And this means that in addition to being as fair as possible, society must also be as merciful as possible.

J

Again, don't take it from us, take it from God: "Do justice, love kindness, and walk humbly with your God" (Micah 6:8).

See also: mercy; righteousness

justification \JUHS-tih-fih-KĀ-shuhn\ n.

The teaching about how we get on God's good side, about how we get "right with God." The "article by which the church stands or falls," meaning that when we don't get this teaching right . . . timber!

Take a look at how the text of this paragraph is laid out. What do you find most noteworthy? No, it's not the type size or line spacing (although those *are* pretty cool). No, we're talking about the fact that this paragraph is "fully justified." The text is lined up along the left-hand margin of the page and along the right-hand margin of the page. Neato! In the typographical sense justification has to do with the alignment of text. In the theological sense justification has to do with God's alignment of you.

"A person is justified by faith apart from works prescribed by the law" (Romans 3:28). Talk about crazy talk! That's about the craziest talk there is, because at the heart of justification is the word *justice*. Now usually when you think about justice, you think about the LAW. So you'd think that justification would be all about the law, or measuring up to some legal standard.

But noooo. Instead right there, smack in the middle of the New Testament, there's this crazy talk of a new, *non-legal* standard for justice—for "gettin' right" with God. What's that you say? You're having a hard time understanding how you can have justice without law? Well, you're not the only one.

Duh: Okay, God, tell me again which rules I have to obey to get on your good side.

God: *You want to get on my good side? Well, then, the first thing you have to do is give up the idea that following rules is going to get you on my good side.*

Duh: No rules?

God: *No rules. Instead, I'll give you my Son, Jesus. He'll take care of all the rules. He'll be the one who makes sure that you're on my good side.*

Duh: But that's just crazy.

God: *Look, you're going to have to trust me on this one . . .*

"Justification by faith apart from works." It's a pretty simple (yet crazy) idea. It's also the most important idea, as far as Christianity is concerned. Many Christians have argued that this crazy talk about justification is the top-dog doctrine of the Christian faith. It's "the article by which the church stands or falls" (or as they say in fancy-schmancy Latin: *articulus stantis et cadensis ecclesia*).

Why is justification the chief article? Because if you get this one right and keep this one right, you're gonna be okay, no matter what else you screw up. (And trust us, you will screw up.) So let's say it again: Ephesians 2:8–9 says that we are saved by grace through faith. Furthermore, this faith is not our own doing. This faith is the gift of God, not the result of works, so that no one may boast about how they were able to work up enough faith to get on God's good side.

Now remind yourself of that every day for the rest of your life. Go ahead and start now, we'll wait.

See also: baptism; Christ (Messiah); faith; free will; gospel; Jesus; law; works, good

kenosis \kih-NOH-sihs\ n.

The idea that Christ is a glass both fully empty and fully . . . well . . . full at the same time.

How do you fit something that is infinite into a finite space or something that is immortal in a mortal body? A shoe horn? Not gonna get the job done. The infinite, immortal, sinless One has to *empty* itself into a finite, mortal body. *Kenosis*, from the Greek word for "empty," describes Christ's emptying of himself (see Philippians 2:7) into human form. How far will Christ go to love and save you? All the way. Christ pours it all out for us until he is empty, thereby making our cup of SALVATION all the way full.

See also: incarnation; Christology; incarnation

kingdom of God (aka reign of God) \KEENG-duhm-uhv-GAHD\ \RĀN-uhv-gahd\ n.

A time that hasn't happened yet but already has begun; a place that doesn't exist yet but where you already live.

As Yoda might have said, "Confused be; very confused be." The kingdom (or reign for those who don't think of God as a male monarch) of God, refers to the time and place where God's will is done. For optimists, God's reign started as Christ's resurrection, when the curtain went up in the drama of God's SALVATION. For pessimists, there is still plenty of against-God's-will sinning going on, so the reign won't start until the curtain goes down at the end of time and all evil is gone. Rest easy— God's reign is both now and not yet. God's Spirit is active, but we also await the end of all suffering.

See also: eschatology; second coming

laity \LĀ-ih-tee\ n. (singular: lay person)

Those people who don't need special degrees, titles, clothes, or roles to know that they are called by God.

Have you heard the one about the pastor, the bishop, the seminary professor, and the lay person arriving together at the pearly gates? St. Peter asked them how they knew they were called by God.

The pastor responded, "I earned a Master of Divinity from my church's most prestigious seminary. Throughout the community people called me either 'pastor' or 'the reverend.' Most days I wore a black shirt with a funny tab where a tie was supposed be. And of course I preached the sermons, did the baptisms, and celebrated the Lord's Supper."

The bishop chimed in, "In addition to my MDiv, I was privileged to receive an honorary doctorate. People called me 'your holiness' or 'your eminence' (except my spouse, who called me 'sweetheart'). On formal worship occasions I wore a special hat called a *miter*. And of course I did all the ordinations."

The seminary professor answered, "I earned a PhD in theology. I was known as 'doctor' or 'professor.' I wore a dated tweed jacket and some old hush puppies. And of course I wrote important books and lectured using big words."

(*If you come from a Christian tradition with such luminary offices as deacon, diaconal minister, nun, monk, elder, patriarch, etc., write your own extra paragraph here.*)

The lay person shook his head and said, "I was baptized in the name of the Father, and of the Son, and of the Holy Spirit."

Go ahead and laugh.

See also: baptism; bishop; muggle; pastor/priest; ordination; vocation

law \law\ n.

God's shalts and shalt-nots,* which seem most directly relevant to someone else's offenses.

Certain things happen. The sun rises. Dogs bark. Water continues to be wet. Human beings seem congenitally prone to speeding,

---

*For those who do not speak the King's English, "dos and don'ts."

stealing, and screwing up. These are, currently, non-negotiable aspects of human existence pending further divine intervention.

In light of these realities, we can think of God's law in a couple of ways: "the way things are" and "the way things ought to be."

Gravity happens. It's part of the God-built world and just goes on working all by itself. Limits imposed by natural laws such as gravity keep the universe orderly and a fairly predictable and stable place to hang out. Messing with these laws has a price (think falls from twenty thousand feet, lobsteresque sunburns, spoiled mayonnaise, etc.). Learn to abide within these boundaries, however, and some amazing things are possible (think powered flight, the bungee cord, the *Saint Tropez* tan, egg salad, etc.). Creation itself, as "the way things are," helps make up a part of what law is. Gravity and the other laws of God's CREATION happen to everybody. These laws are impersonal. It's as easy to drink as drown in wet water.

God's will isn't only cleverly built into the structures of creation, however. God isn't content to wind up the world and let it putter along purely according to the laws of physics. God is *interested* in us and involved in an ongoing relationship with the world and its occupants. God refuses to be indifferent to nonmathematical realities like infidelity and injustice. God demands that we treat ourselves and one another well. God's will for "the way things ought to be," revealed in the Old and New Testaments, is the second half of what law means in a theological conversation.

Despite our long and productive group effort at perfecting human sin, God loves the world and wants all of creation to flourish. God gives us the law because God loves us—all of us—and if we will all follow God's laws, we will all thrive. The dos and don'ts that make up the Ten Commandments (for example) highlight and define the boundaries of a healthy people, a functional society, and even a thriving ecology and economy—God's desire for everyone and everything.

The Ten Commandments, and God's intentions standing behind them, form the moral core of biblically based ethics. These commandments gave the prophets such strong traction against the people of Israel. And they continue both to guide and irritate us today. Just like gravity, God's vision and will for "the way things ought to be" still applies to us, whether we ignore it or not.

See also: creation; Decalogue; fall, the; sin

law, uses of the \yoo-sihz-uhv-thuh-LAW\ n.

The two-headed push-me-pull-me (or three-headed dragon, for *Game of Thrones* fans) of the theological menagerie.

There are two widely agreed ways that God uses the LAW (and a third way that is highly debated). Theologians call these the *uses of the law*.

1. The civil use of the law*

To understand the civil use, think about a loving mother's rules for her children: "Hey, don't bash your brother over the head with that rock! And you, don't poke your sister in the eye with that stick!" The kids reply, "Is that a rule for just right now? Or is that forever a rule as in forever?" Mother just sighs.

Now why would a mother make rules like that? Obviously, it is because Mom loves both of her kids, unlovable as they sometimes might be.

God's civil use of the law trains everyone to behave as civilly as possible; indeed, it makes the world more civil. The use of the law is all the more important given our human predilection toward suckiness. Our suckiness means that we don't fit perfectly into our own bodies. The first use, then, is like a belt used to hold up a pair of pants that don't fit quite right; it helps everything stay in place (unless you are a plumber, in which case we wish you would wear overalls).

Trouble starts a-brewin' however, when we get it into our heads that following and obeying all of these cool laws earns us a high credit rating, platinum card, and travel-reward points with the Almighty. When it comes to getting into heaven, God doesn't take plastic (or

_____

*To make matters more confusing—which is what theologians always try to do—Lutherans call the civil use of the law "the first use of the law," while Reformed Christians call the civil use of the law "the second use of the law."

personal checks). The law ain't no savior. The law cannot be used to make oneself right with God.

2. The theological use of the law*

If the first use of the law is like a belt, the second use of the law is more like a mirror or a flashlight. God shines the law into our lives in order to highlight the embarrassing gap between what God wants and the fact every single one of us falls short of God's hopes. Like a flashlight on your great uncle Kenny early in the morning before he has put in his teeth or put on his fake hair, the law shows us the truth about ourselves. And the truth is, we fail to love God with all our heart, soul, and mind, and we also fail to love our neighbor as ourselves. Although in our defense, we never did bash our little brother over the head with that rock.

God uses the law to confront us and teach us that we need to repent and that we need God's FORGIVENESS, GRACE, and LOVE. Though we don't always fully comprehend the magnitude of our failures, the law helps us get a sense of how much we suck and how much we would rather not suck.

Interlude: The Gospel

---

*You guessed it, Lutherans call the theological use of the law "the second use of the law," while Reformed Christians call the theological use of the law "the first use of the law." In Lutherans' defense, Luther invented the numbers, and Calvin just copied and renumbered.

Peas have carrots, Batman has Robin, peanut butter has jelly. The Law's partner is the gospel. As the second use of the law makes us conscious of our need for SALVATION, so the gospel fills that need and gives us back the law in its first use—as a gift from God to order and bless all of CREATION. See the entire entry GOSPEL.

3. The disputed third (or pedagogical) use of the law*

In the first edition of *Crazy Talk*, we did not include any mentioned of the third use of the law because, well, there isn't one. Being hyper-Lutheran friends, we just don't get it. Sorry. Not really. But the famous Old Testament theologian Walter Brueggemann (WB), who is much nicer than we are, wrote us a kind note.

WB: "When it comes to a second edition of *Crazy Talk*, consider inviting a Reformed theologian to write on the third use of the law."

Us: "What is the third use of the law?"

WB: "The commandments are God's gift to God's people; they voice the substantive expectations of faithful covenant and so function for the redeemed who gladly obey them as a mandate as a way

---

*Lutherans and Reformed Christian both agree that the third use of the law is third. However, just to be difficult, not all Lutherans believe in the third use of the law (because in the official book of Lutheran teachings, some documents speak of two uses of the law and others speak of three). In addition—we wish we were making this up—Lutherans and Reformed theologians that do believe in the third use of the law define it a little differently.

to live well and responsibly in a new covenantal relationship. Christians, like Jews, can find joy in the Torah, for the commandments are a disclosure of what new God-given life looks like. They permit a life answered back to God in gratitude."

Us: "We love that! Except we think that is still the first use of the law. You are focusing on the human beings as the user of the law; we are focusing on God using the law. We agree that people—all people, not just God's covenant people—can love God's law and love keeping rules and commandments. But since we are focusing on God as the user of the Law, we still only see two uses of the law. But we love you. In a first use of the law kind of way."

Cue soundtrack: Meatloaf, "Two Out of Three Ain't Bad."

See also: gospel; justification; salvation; sin

logos \LOH-gohs\ n.

The single block that holds all reality together. Not to be confused with the tiny, colorful, snap-together bricks used in the construction of trucks, spaceships, and castles.

A Greek word that means "word" or "reason" or "purpose," this term enters the *Crazy Talk* lexicon most clearly in the opening verses of the Gospel of John, where the author recounts the biblical creation story, starting with "the Word" (see John 1:1–4): the Word is Jesus Christ, God's self in flesh and blood. God has spoken a word of love and life to the entire world, and the name of this Word is Jesus.

See also: Christ (Messiah); creation; Jesus; Trinity

love \luhv\ n.

Not a thing that is blind, but the act of actually seeing the needs of others.

You can't love your car. Or your house. Or your rubber ducky. Your car/house/ducky may be nicer than any of ours, but if you "love" them, you're really just loving what you have—thus you are just being devoted to your own self, your own pleasure, and your own happiness. If you think you love your car, you need a whack upside the head and a serious reevaluation of priorities.

Love is not a sentiment or an emotion. It is not something you feel but action you take on behalf of others. And love certainly isn't blind. Love stares the suffering and needs of the NEIGHBOR hard in the face. And then it does something about them.

If you have a problem with this, you might have a problem with God. And if you think you might go all tricksy-lawyer with God and quibble by asking, "Exactly who is my neighbor?," that line of thought has already been tried and failed (see Luke 10:25–37).

We are only able to love because God first loved us (see 1 John 3:16). God's very nature is love, since God's actions of CREATION, REDEMPTION, and SANCTIFICATION are continuous acts of love. Seeing as the world doesn't stop existing for people who are jerks, we can know that God's love is unconditional.

See also: anger of God; attributes of God; grace; works, good

martyr \MAR-tuhr\ n.

A person who would rather die than allow you to help make dinner.

Chances are you think you know one. These are the dear souls in your life who make a point of letting everyone within earshot know how hard they work to make others comfortable and happy, how they perpetually work those fingers to the proverbial bone in thankless and selfless pursuits, all the while stoically (and loudly) asserting, "It's nothing . . ."

If this is what springs to mind when you hear the word *martyr*, it's time to move out of your parents' house, get a job, and start washing your own laundry. And no, even this act of responsible self-sacrifice won't make you a martyr.

From the Greek word for "testimony," as given in a court by an eyewitness to an event, the word *martyr* was used by early Christians to describe those whose were willing to be put to death rather than take back their WITNESS to Jesus. The martyr's flesh was where the active witness to Jesus Christ met the sword-poking and fire-breathing feedback of the various lords who took offense at this faithful Christian CONFESSION.

M

Don't try this at home, kids. Among Christians the vocation of martyr is not to be pursued zealously, but it is also not to be fled from in panic. Martyrs are those who were unwilling to save their own skins and thereby helped to ensure that you got a chance to hear the good news that God is love.

See also: cross; disciple; worship

means of grace \MEEN-**zuhv**-GRĀS\ n.

The simplest everyday stuff through which the most profound event of eternity happens to you.

Have you ever *smelled* cold or hot? Have you ever *felt* a scream? How can a person see that which is invisible or hold that which has no substance in one's hands? That is what the *means of grace* are all about. God's grace—God's Redeeming Actions Concerning Everyone—is an event that frees us, forgives us, empowers us. But how does it come to us? In the simplest everyday things: words, water, bread, wine, and community. In the Word of God, the sacraments of BAPTISM and COMMUNION, and in the community of the CHURCH, God's GRACE can he smelled, felt, seen, heard, held, and tasted.

See also: Bible; sacrament; Word of God

M

member \MEHM-**buhr**\ n.

One who joins a group in order to avoid expectations of participation; God's partner in mission.

There are all kinds of church members—every-week worshipers; 10-percent tithers; once-a-month communion munchers; showers-up for the annual picnic or golf tournament; and our personal favorites, CEO Christians: they show for *C*hristmas, *E*aster and *O*ne other Sunday (and probably for grandma's funeral, but this is optional).

Sometimes it seems that members do less and show less than folks who haven't yet joined the group. That may be true of some, but to be fair, it's just as true that once someone joins the group, the church sometimes pays them less attention.

In the New Testament there isn't actually much "member/membership" talk. First Corinthians 12 has the most, and that bit of Paul is one big metaphor: here a "member" is not a "joiner" but a body part. Paul talks about hands, feet, ears, and eyes (very little talk of the nose, although why Paul wouldn't pick it . . . ha ha ha) and how they all have a place in the choir—to make a mess of the metaphor.

A better way to think about what a member is would be to think about every member as God's partner. God is on a mission to love, save, and bless the world. Every church is a group of people committed to that MISSION. When you join a church, God says, "You are now my partner in the effort to love, save, and bless the whole world."

This includes you and every other member: armpit or big toe, tither or CEO.

See also: Christian; disciple

mercy \MUHR-see\ n.

A quality we think of as indicating weakness in human beings but in fact shows strength in and from God; a knuckle-interlocking game that leads to prayer.

One of our favorite times of the year is state fair time—when the kids are almost back in school (hallelujah!), roller-coaster and human-sling-shooting rides come to town (good God almighty!), and we eat three meals within the space of three hours, all on a stick (why, O Lord?). But the best thing about the fair is the judging. Horses, cows, quilts, pies, wood carving—you name it, they judge it at the fair. Even people get judged. There is the fair queen (which is different than the fair lady), and of course there are all of the people silently sizing up and judging each other.

And then there is God. Who is not fair. And that, friend, is the good news.

M

Instead, God is merciful. God's mercy is all about *unfairness*. If God treated us as fairness demanded, we'd be in some serious trouble. If God collected from us every time we fell behind on our accounts, we'd be permanently spiritually bankrupt (if you catch our drift). If God held it against us every time we worshiped our idols of money, career, family, war, or sex, we'd be forgotten forever (so to speak). If God brought charges against us each time we ignored the widow or orphan, we'd be serving multiple eternal life sentences (concurrently).

But God isn't fair; God is merciful.

Mercy is who God is. Because of God's mercy, we can run to our Creator, not hide—no matter what we've done or failed to do. We can "return to the Lord, our God, for he is gracious and merciful, slow to anger and abounding in steadfast love, and relents from punishing" (Joel 2:13).

So does that mean that God is some big wimp? When human beings show mercy, we tend to think it is a sign of weakness. If a banker forgives loans every time she feels sorry for a customer who is behind on a payment, the bank would go under. If a teacher forgives an assignment every time he feels bad for the kid whose dog ate the homework, the poor kid would not learn.

But in God, mercy actually shows God's strength. Think of it this way. When a husband and wife argue, the one who forgives the other first is actually the one with the stronger character. When two friends have a falling out, the one who calls to patch things up is the one with inner strength.

And that is who God is. We rebelled against God, crucified his Son, and rejected his teaching. And God said, "I forgive, I raise Jesus up for you, and I won't abandon you. Because I am merciful and gracious, slow to anger and abounding in steadfast love" (see Exodus 34:6).

See also: anger of God; attributes of God; forgiveness; justice; love

ministry \MIH-nih-stree\ n.

An office instituted by God for work in God's world, the holders of which often spend too much time in their offices.

With an unfortunate assonance with *misery*, the office of *ministry* was instituted by God for the alleviation of misery but, unfortunately, sometimes causes it. The purpose of the office is to minister to the needs of others, to love, save, and bless the world. Sadly, the temptation is for holders of the office to see first to the needs of the office. But here is the incredibly good news—God has chosen to use sinners in order to love, save, and bless the world. This means we are all qualified for ministry.

M

See also: bishop; laity; pastor/priest; vocation

miracle \MEER-uh-kuhl\ n.

An occurrence that seems impossible and supernatural from a human perspective; an occurrence that, from a divine perspective, ain't nothin' but a thing.

"Everything has a natural explanation," the more scientifically minded will want to tell us.

This is true, since godly intervention is, in fact, quite natural—after all, God created nature. Miracles are not predictable or measurable—at least not according to the standards of science, which doesn't see them as "real." But as far as God is concerned, miracles are part of reality. Maybe God even prefers being a bit unpredictable. But don't take our word for it, or even the word of Scripture. Just ask believers if there's such a thing as miracles, and see what kind of answers you get.

P.S. You may think it is a miracle when your little brother finally gets a date, but actually, this is just desperation and pity.

See also: angel; experience; prayer

mission \MIH-shuhn\ n.

The greatest party ever; what God is up to for you, your neighbor, and all creation; your participation and presence are boldly requested.

An Invitation

Who: You (and every other sinner).

What: God's mission to love, save, bless, and free all of creation from the power of sin. It is a party of cosmic proportions and ultimate significance. And joy.

When: Now and 'til the cows come home, all the colors bleed into one (copyright U2), and time quits tickin'.

Where: Wherever the power of sin is causing bondage, despair, brokenness, loneliness, meaninglessness, sinfulness, and many
other kinds of -ness. Groups are meeting in local congregations, homes, and on the street.

Bring: Your God-given gifts and talents. Come as you are, but
expect to be changed. No special attire is required, but you
may find yourself going an extra mile, sharing an extra coat,
or offering your NEIGHBOR a cup of cool water in Christ's
name.

R.S.V.P. requested. Please contact the Father, Son, and Holy Spirit.

See also: church; disciple

money \MUH-nee\ n. (aka mammon, lucre, moolah, cash, Benjamins)

M

Your true god, unless you remember that it belongs first to God.

"Aha!" you gasp. "I've got this one! I don't need money defined for
me! I know what to say about money! The Bible says that money is
the root of all evil. I'm smarter than you, theology person!" That's
really nice, but allow us to one-up you. Take a look back at the passage to which you likely refer, and marvel that it actually claims
that the *love* of money is the root of all evil. Money on its own isn't
inherently bad. Adoring it and chasing it at any cost is pretty darned
expensive—at least spiritually expensive. Money makes a great tool
but a really terrible master.

Jesus talked about money a lot. Like, a *lot*. Probably more than you think your pastor does, and you probably think your pastor talks about money basically any time you show up at church. Is there ever not a stewardship drive going on? What are they, NPR?

Anyway, you don't have to believe us, but there's a good reason Jesus talked way more about money than he did about sex: we must put money into context in our Christian lives. Your bank statement reveals something about your faith. If someone looked at your credit card bill, could they tell you are a Christian? If not, it might be time to examine whether you worship money more than you worship God.

"God cares about what you do with *all* your money—not just the part that you give away to God." Just stop and think about that little gem of crazy talk for a minute.

M

Ultimately, we must understand money to be just another tool in our life of faith. We use money, just like our time, talent, possessions, and relationships, in order to serve God and our neighbors. When we lose sight of that—when we pursue it for its own sake, when it rules all our choices and identity—it might be time to consider that the God in which you trust is actually the currency itself. We're pretty sure that breaks a commandment or something.

See also: idol

monotheism \MAH-noh-THEE-ih-zuhm\ n.

The practice of worshiping one god (not counting the one in the mirror).

In terms of number, theisms are a lot like ice cream. Some people prefer one flavor at a time, while others are the-more-the-merrier kind of folk. The monotheists profess faith in one single deity, most often called God. The most easily recognizable monotheists are Jews, Muslims, and Christians, although Jews and Muslims sometimes accuse Christians of going Neapolitan (three flavors in one scoop).

See also: heresy; hypostatic union; Trinity

M

N

neighbor \NĀ-buhr\ n.

Who you see when you look everywhere but in a mirror.

In response to the command to love the neighbor, a lawyer asked Jesus, "Who is my neighbor?" Can't blame him; we'd like to pick and choose whom we have to love, too.

Here is God's answer: everyone. Yes, the person who lives in the house next door is our neighbor. So is the family who lives twelve miles out of town, the elderly person in New York, and the teenager in Malawi. And if there's anything to those "Men in Black" movies, maybe our neighbor even includes those extraterrestrial refugees living in our midst.

There are natural boundaries everywhere: mountain ranges, rivers, oceans. As humans, we're quick to construct even more boundaries: fences, state lines, national borders. Though boundaries have their places (literally), they often limit our interactions with our neighbors. God's LOVE knows no boundaries, and God expects our love to know no boundaries, either.

Jesus pushes us beyond our boundaries to respect, assist, and love all people—those within and beyond our confines. It's easy to be neighborly toward family members (most of the time), friends, and pleasant acquaintances, but Jesus has the gall to ask us to consider those who live outside our boundaries, whether they live "across the tracks" or in distant lands. Heck, Jesus even asks us to think of our enemies as neighbors! Who does Jesus think he is? Mr. Rogers?!

See also: ethics; mission

offering \ᴀʜ-**fuhr-eeng**\ n.

That which doesn't really belong to us in the first place and which, often only after much anguished deliberation and wringing of hands, we reluctantly part with as a "gift" to God—presumably in thanks for having given it to us in the first place.

There's an old saying common among pre-schoolers and Australian seagulls (much the same thing, of course): "*Mine! Mine! Mine! Mine! Mine! Mine!*" In a different way, this is true of all we have—ourselves, our time, our possessions . . . food, clothing, home, family, cash, all that we need from day to day. We think that all of it is ours and that it belongs to us. But really it is all a gift from God.

Now here's the crazy thing—God doesn't want those shoes back; God doesn't need your allowance or a pie (it says so in Psalm 50:12–14). Offerings to God are about something different. They're about being thankful and about having our hearts in the right place.

So think of it this way: *"Thank you! Thank you! Thank you! Thank you!"* God gives to us richly and thus makes it possible for us to give richly—back to God for our friends, family, and neighbors (see NEIGHBOR to find out who they are) and for all who are in need. You might say that this is why we have what we have: so that we can offer it to others.

One last thing. You know that year-old can of lima beans given to the local food shelf? That isn't an offering. It's just kind of mean.

See also: love; sacrifice; thanksgiving

omnipotence \ahm-NIH-puh-tuhnts\ n.

The idea that God is powerful enough both to overpower all resistance and to save the world without doing so.

Question: Can God create a rock so big that God can't lift it? Answer: There are no stupid questions, only stupid people who ask questions. God's *omnipotence* means that God is all powerful. Unfortunately—or fortunately—for us, God's limitless power surpasses our ability to understand it. Does God's omnipotence mean we are just puppets? Does the existence of suffering mean an all-powerful God doesn't care? The Bible says that God proves God's ultimate power in becoming weak enough to die on the cross for us.

See also: omnipresence; omniscience

omnipresence \ahm-nih-PREH-zihnts\ n.

The idea that God is so big that the universe can't contain God yet small enough to dwell even in your heart.

As the argument goes, God is beyond us because God can be everywhere all at once. Nonetheless, most of us have experienced times and places that seem distinctly out of God's presence. Plus, if God is everywhere, we might be tempted to think that God is a tree or a bird, when those things are God's CREATION but not God incarnate (see INCARNATION). Instead, it means that there is no place or time that is out of God's sight, making us never truly alone. Everything that exists reminds us of that PROMISE. A comforting thought, unless you like getting into trouble.

See also: omnipotence; omniscience; transcendence of God

omniscience \ahm-NIH-shuhnts\ n.

The idea that God knows all, including, one supposes, knowing what isn't worth knowing.

If you know what isn't worth knowing, do you really know everything? This word means that God is all knowing; it means that God sees us, our lives, and all of time in one single, solitary blink of light. In the Bible, for every Jeremiah 29:11 where God knows your whole life, there's a Jonah 3:10, where God's mind was changed. If God knew God's mind would change, was it really changed? Our brains hurt. Just know this: there is nowhere and no-when you can go that God cannot rescue you (see Psalm 139).

See also: free will; omnipotence; omnipresence

ontology \ahn-TAH-luh-jee\ n.

Metaphysical reflection on the qualitative difference between the essence of various entities, for instance, margarine and butter.

As with the other -ologies we've covered, *Crazy Talk* seeks to define that which is partly indescribable. You can sum up *ontology* by the common-sense observation, "If it ain't one thing, it's another." *Ontology* considers when a difference between two things is a matter of essence or a matter of appearance (which theologians call "accidents"—but don't ask why). A simple theological example is the difference between God and a human being. These two are ontologically (notice the adverbial use) different—even more unlike than butter and margarine.

You'll be reassured to know that nobody has a full-time job as an ontologist (at least not a paid one).

Some people suggest that males and females are ontologically different from one another. We don't have a dog in that fight, although we will observe both that dogs are ontologically different from cats and that for women, going to the restroom is a team sport, while for men it is an individual one.

Some church types suggest that "ontological change" is possible among human beings through the working of God. For example,

some suggest that both BAPTISM and ORDINATION create ontological change, and thus Christians are ontologically different from non-Christians and pastors are different than lay people. We don't buy this.

The major ontological line is the one between humanity and God. Sacraments like baptism and rites such as ordination do not change who we are (our essence); they change *whose* we are (our relationships).

See also: attributes of God; pastor/priest; sacrament; sanctification; theology

ordination \ohr-dih-NĀ-shuhn\ n.

A ceremony of God's church during which someone God has called is consecrated for God's ministry on behalf of God's world—and so, naturally, people who are ordained think that it is all about them.

Thank you for reading this entry. Most folks don't give a rip about the particulars of bureaucratic processes and human resource concerns. To a large extent, that's what ordination amounts to, with the added veneer of church ritual and religio-speak, of course. We're not trying to be flip. It's just that all pastors-to-be are sinners just like us.

Too often, ordination is set up in such a way that the pastor-to-be is placed high up on a spiritual pedestal. The resulting high hopes, coupled with the pastor's natural flaws, inevitably produce disenchantment, burnout, and worse. It's one thing for a church to have a bit of a celebration when one from their midst is being lifted up as public preacher of the gospel. It's another thing to (a) set someone up for failure or (b) believe your own publicity.

It'd be chaotic if just anybody could get up in a pulpit and let fly. So a little order for the preaching office is, well, in order. Ordination sets aside those people who the CHURCH believes are divinely called and thoroughly prepared for MINISTRY.

On the other hand, ordained pastors do well to remember that it's not about them. Ordination is about what God is doing through the preaching, teaching, and ministry of everyday sinners.

See also: mission; ontology; pastor/priest; vocation

163

orthodox \ohr-thuh-dahks\ adj.

Pertaining to those who color inside the lines using only the right hand and approved colors.

Coming from the Greek words *orthos* ("right") and *doxa* ("opinion"), to be *orthodox* means to do or believe correctly. In many spheres of life, right and wrong do not apply. There is no right side of the bread to butter and no right side of your head on which to part your hair— the left just often looks better. Likewise, there is no right style of music for worship. Orthodoxy is best applied to DOCTRINE, CONFESSION of faith, spiritual-mindedness (see Psalm 51), and rooting for particular baseball teams.

See also: adiaphora; dogma; heresy

Orthodox Church \ohr-thuh-dahkx-chuhrch\ n.

The eastern half of the Christian church that the Western church usually forgets about completely.

You can't make this stuff up. In 1054 CE, for reasons that we cannot even begin to review, the Bishop of Rome—a little someone we like to call "the pope"—sent a letter excommunicating the Bishop of Constantinople—a little someone we like to call "the patriarch." In response, the Bishop of Constantinople excommunicated the pope's representatives who brought the letter.

Known as the "Great Schism," the events of 1054 caused churches around the Mediterranean to choose sides once and for all. Either you were with Rome (hence Roman Catholic), or you were with Constantinople (Eastern Orthodox).

There are a variety of "orthodox churches"—Russian Orthodox, Greek Orthodox, Serbian Orthodox, and so on—although they consider themselves "one CHURCH." Orthodox churches are governed by bishops and characterized by their strict adherence to the teachings of the seven ecumenical church councils.

See also: Catholic; council; Protestant; excommunication

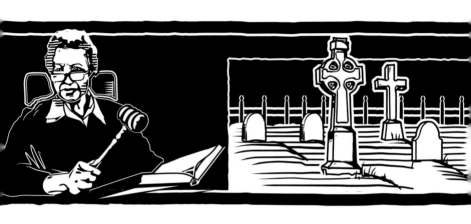

pastor/priest \PA-**stuhr** / **preest**\ n.

A sinner who is so aware of the power of sin in his or her own life that he or she feels called by the Holy Spirit to announce that God loves sinners.

The guys in Duh's barbershop were jibbering away, laughing at Duh's off-color jokes, when a new guy came in. (Note: This story could just as easily take place in a hair salon, into which a new woman walks, but Duh is a guy. If you haven't met Duh, see the entry on GOD.) The four-letter-filled, dirty-joke tellin', locker-room chatter went on until it was the new guy's turn in the chair.

Duh asked, "New in town or just passing through?"

"I'm new," came the response.

"That's wonderful! What do you do?"

"I'm the new pastor up at Our Savior's," said the pastor.

That's wonderful, Duh groaned to himself, *that's where I go to church.* Three men, suddenly remembering that their sprinklers were running, headed out the door.

Here is the first thing that you need to know about pastors: they are sinners just like you are. In fact, the reason they became pastors is that they knew the power of SIN in their own lives so intimately that they wanted to preach the LOVE, FORGIVENESS, and the power of God full time.

Here's a second thing about pastors: you need one. Sure, the Holy Spirit gives gifts to everyone. And sure, we are all called to be everyday ministers of God. But God has established a particular MINISTRY—known as the ministry of word and SACRAMENT—and God has called men and women to this ministry. Why? Because the world needs regular and responsible preaching. And the sacraments need regular and responsible administering. By *word*, we mean the proclamation that Jesus loves and saves sinners (not perfect people). By *sacrament*, we mean baptisms and Holy Communion, which are visible works. Without word and sacrament, the CHURCH would just be a nice theory. With them, the church is a hearable, tasteable, feelable reality.

Spend any time around pastor-types, and the word "call" will surface faster than a speeding bullet. Call is certainly important to ordained ministry. The call is two-fold. Pastors are called by (1) the Holy Spirit and (2) the community of faith. We set apart those called to leadership by a service of ORDINATION. In the service the candidate promises to be faithful to Christ and to the whole people of God.

But aren't pastors perfect saints, incredible preachers, foolproof counselors, visionary leaders, always in control, with a certain faith that always has the answer to any question? One word: not on your life. Okay, that was four words. But you get the point.

And one more thing. Never WORSHIP your pastor. Worship Jesus. You don't go to church to hear your pastor; you go to church to hear your pastor preach Jesus.

See also: sermon; vocation

Pentecost \PEHN-tih-kawst\ n.

A great name for a '57 Chevy convertible, the birthday of the church, or the longest, most ordinary time of the church year.

Pop quiz: What are the three major festivals of the church year?

And your answer is . . .

Okay, forget for a second that you are reading an entry on "Pentecost." If you weren't, would you have named Christmas, Easter, and Pentecost? Really? With God as your witness?

Speaking of witness, Pentecost is all about witness . . . and *fire*!

Pentecost was the day that the Holy Spirit came and lit a fire—quite literally (read all about it in Acts 2)—under the witness of the church. On the day of Pentecost—fifty days after the first Easter—tongues of fire appeared on the disciples' heads. The disciples were filled with the Holy Spirit, and they began witnessing to Christ. Some people refer to this day as the birthday of the church.

Each year the church celebrates its birthday—that is, the day the Holy Spirit came and lit a fire in us—by marking the festival of Pentecost. The church also celebrates the season of Pentecost, which lasts from the Day of Pentecost until the first Sunday of Advent. It is the longest season of the church year.

See also: church; Holy Spirit; tongues (speaking in); witness

perichoresis \PEHR-ee-kuh-REE-sihs\ n.

The attempt to describe the numbers "three" and "one" without using math.

Q: Who is God?

A: God is TRINITY, three persons in one God.

Q: Does that add up?

A: Yes, each of these persons shares of the same divine substance and yet is a separate person—the Father and Son are separate and yet they dwell in each other through the Holy Spirit.

Q: Isn't that crazy talk?

A: Yes, it's *perichoresis*, to be specific, which means the three persons of the Trinity "indwell" the others. The three persons live in, with, and through each other. *Perichoresis* maintains the tension between the unity and the threeness of the Trinity. It affirms community (without conformity) and personality (without isolation).

See also: Trinity

person \PUHR-suhn\ n.

Not to be confused with the son of Per (who is not a bad guy); one part "image of God" + one part dirt + one part spirit + one part speech + one part broken + one part beloved = a person.

Have you ever actually thought about what a person is? We mean, you are one—the very fact that you are interacting with these words means you are a person. Humans alone have the gift of language— or, at least, advanced language (or as we fancy theologians call it, "talk"). Your family pet might know fifty or so simple words, but you can talk yourself into circles, with conjunction junctions, subordinate Clauses (or "elves," as we like to call them), dangling prepositions, split infinitives, and sentence fragments. Whether you are moving your lips as you read these words or speak fluently and read way beyond your grade level, being a person means being shaped by word and story. As Elie Wiesel said, "God made man because God loves stories."

The Bible describes what a person is in many several different ways. First, the Bible says that all human beings, regardless of gender, are created in the "image of God" (Genesis 1:26). Go read what we said about that, because we worded real good about that one already. But trust us: it is pretty cool to know that you are a spittin' image of your Creator!

In Genesis 2:7, the Good Book says that "the LORD God formed the human from the dirt of the ground, and breathed into his nostrils the breath of life; and the man became a living being." God built humans out of more than thoughts, ideas, and pixie dust. Basically, our tangible, physical selves are no more glamorous than what you vacuum out of your carpet. And yet we have God's breath in us. You are flesh, and you are a spiritual being!

But there is some sad news. We are all also broken. Genesis 3 tells the story of "the fall," how we are all born into the condition of "sin" (which is to say, we are all born into suckitude). Our bodies fail. We make deadly mistakes. We do evil. Or, as St. Paul said, "I do not do what I want, but I do the very thing I hate" (Romans 7:15). Sorry to have to say this, but cute and wonderful as you are, you are broken. You sin. And one day you will die. Everything will. Feel free to stare blankly into the middle distance as you ponder how much this ruined your day.

But come on back, because there is one more thing. You are loved. In particular, you are loved by your Creator so intensely much that God took on flesh and blood just like yours, "moved into the neighborhood" (copyright Eugene Peterson), and died so that you may be a new creation. "God so loved the world that God gave his only begotten Son so that everyone who believes in him may not perish but have eternal life" (John 3:16). If being a person is good enough for God, we think you can make it work, too.

See also: anthropology; creation; fall, the; image of God; incarnation; sin

pilgrimage \PIL-gruh-mij\ n.

(1) Not to be confused with pill + grim + age—the uninviting medicinal tablets many senior citizens swallow—a journey people take when they are trying to find either themselves or God; (2) life itself.

A religious pilgrimage is a journey to a holy site, most often taken in hopes of connecting more deeply with God. Some take these journeys because they want an immersive experience of God. Others hope for a transcendent moment of personal or spiritual discovery. Others have been sold on a trip only offered because the pastor wanted to fly for free.

Getting out of your regular routine invites you into a new perspective, like how visiting your sister and her little urchins makes your own kids look like saints. A pilgrimage can offer this sort of experience.

Better yet, some Christians believe that certain places offer a more ready encounter with God. Celtic Christians speak of "thin places," where the veil between heaven and earth is a little more like Swiss cheese and less like a good, hard cheddar. Some other Christians believe that holy items (called "relics" in the theology business), often located at pilgrimage sites, allow you to basically look through that gap and sneak a peek at the divine. Some of the more famous Christian pilgrimage sites are

The Holy Land (especially Jerusalem)
Rome (especially St. Peter's Basilica)
Mt. Sinai (St Catherine's Monastery)
Ireland (Croagh Patrick Chapel)
Mexico (Basilica of Our Lady of Guadalupe)
The Nearest Ikea (at least until you've tried to assemble a bed)

Still other Christians think it's just about the journey. As in, all of life is a journey, a pilgrimage of faith—a long journey from the cradle to the grave, at the end of which we will be met by God. You know, "life is a highway" theology. It's only cliché because it's true. The book of Hebrews encourages us to run life's pilgrimage as if it were a marathon: "Let us run with perseverance the race that is set before us, looking to Jesus the pioneer and perfecter of our faith (Hebrews 12:1–2). Every day we journey through and to the divine.

And for some of us, as we continue to walk the pilgrimage of faith, we need a couple of ibuprofen, or at least a well-placed bench.

See also: faith; holy & holiness; Holy Spirit; cheese

pneumatology \noo-muh-ᴛᴀʜ-luh-jee\ n.

The study of the ineffable third member of the Trinity expressed through the thoroughly effable medium of words.

From the words *pneuma* (bless you!), meaning "Spirit," and ʟᴏɢᴏs, meaning "word," pneumatology is the study of the Spirit. Since the Spirit blows when and where it wants (see John 3:8), one can't set up a field lab to study it. The "lab" of the Spirit, therefore, is the life of the believer—in whom and through whom the Spirit works. The Spirit creates ꜰᴀɪᴛʜ (1 Corinthians 12:3), gives gifts (1 Corinthians 11–12), bears fruit in a believer's life (Galatians 5:22–23), creates community and consolation (Philippians 2:1), and so on. That's a lot to study.

See also: Holy Spirit; Pentecost

praise \prāz\ v.

To give credit to God—often through song, chant, and other tortured forms of expression—for things that we secretly believe we did for ourselves.

If you are like us, the very thought of praise may just give you the creeps. "To praise" may invoke thoughts of sweaty, barbeque-fed worshipers in a too-close assembly, raising their hands in the air and singing Jesus-is-my-boyfriend types of songs. Or it may drag back long-repressed memories of Bible camp campfires and your best friend feeling the need to hug you. We give you permission at this point to shiver.

In fact, you may think that praise is profoundly *unnatural*—and you would be right! Praise is unnatural because praising God gives God credit for everything that God has done for you, for those you love, and for the world.

And just think about how *unnatural* that truly is. Why? Because sinners—and that includes all of us—want to take credit for ourselves. And how do we do this? We say "congratulations" to each other.

New baby? "Congratulations!" (Meaning, "Good job, you deserve all the credit.") New job? "Congratulations!" Recover from illness? "Congratulations!"

Praise is different. To praise God means that God gets the credit— and it means that we are just the recipients of God's grace. New baby? New job? Renewed health? "Praise the Lord!"

So before praise is anything creepy, it is the most profound way in daily life to express your FAITH. So next time someone shares good news with you, don't say congratulations; say, "Praise the Lord!"

See also: blessing; glory; offering; thanksgiving

P

prayer \prehr\ n.

A form of talking that is often forced on children before bed under the assumption that they ought to be introduced to God before they have a really serious need.

The next time someone says, "You haven't got a prayer," you can tell them, "I got tons of them!" Because the Bible's filled with prayers, and they're all there for you to pray. There are prayers of PRAISE ("Glory to you, O God"), prayers of THANKSGIVING ("Thanks, God"), prayers of CONFESSION ("Forgive me, God"), prayers of lament ("Where are you, God?"), prayers of supplication ("God, here's what I need . . ."), prayers of intercession ("God, here's what my neighbor needs . . ."), and even prayers of listening ("God, here is what we think you are saying").

There's also the Lord's Prayer, a prayer that's considered kind of special because, well, Jesus owns the copyright on it. But don't worry, you can use that one, too!

Simply put, prayer is talking with God. Think about the relationships in your life—with your spouse, your kids, your parents, your mail carrier, your friends, your plants, and so on. Whether it's in

person, via email, or text messaging, communication is crucial to relationships. That's true with God, too. You can talk to God about things as small as the meal in front of you (if you are on a diet and eating smaller portions) and about things as big as your mother's struggle with cancer.

Here are some prayer basics.

Promise. We pray because God has promised to listen. In fact, we pray because God has commanded us to pray *and* promised to listen.

176

To. We pray to God. Prayer doesn't involve just getting things off our chests or out in the open. We pray to God because God just might decide to answer our prayers.

Sorts. See above. There are all sorts of prayers. You can pray about anything you want. Frankly, we've always considered the prayers for parking spaces or for victory in a ballgame kind of silly, but we're not God—which is good for all concerned.

When, where, and how. The Bible says pray all the time, pray in private, pray when you're together as a CHURCH, and don't heap up so many words trying to make your prayers sound impressive. (Take that, pastors!) Prayer doesn't need to be formal. You don't need to pull out and polish the twenty-five-cent words in your vocab. (Besides, who really knows what *obstreperous* means?) You don't need to make it long and boring. (If your pastor is horribly boring, feel free to share this information.) You just need to talk.

Still need a little help? You've probably figured it out by now, but there's no one right way to pray. However, if a guide is helpful, you can remember the acronym ACTS: Adoration, Confession, Thanksgiving, and Supplication. When you begin a prayer in adoration, you praise God for who God is. In confession, you claim who you are as a sinner and ask for FORGIVENESS. For thanksgiving, you identify those gifts for which you are grateful. The prayer closes in supplication—with your pleas, requests, and petitions.

And here is a good way to end: Amen.

See also: blessing; worship

predestination \PREE-deh-stih-NĀ-shuhn\ n.

The extremely disturbing idea that God actually knows what God is doing.

You were predestined to read these words. You only think that you are reading these words by exercising your FREE WILL. But in reality, long ago, it was determined that you would be reading these words right here, right now.

Many sanities have been shipwrecked on the rocky shores of *predestination*. At the very least, people who have thought long and hard about predestination report an increase in headaches and puking. From a human perspective, it's hard to get around the idea of predestination. Follow this recipe: one part all-knowing, all-powerful, all-saving God + one part broken and fallen humanity. Mix together and you might get the idea that God knows ahead of time who will be saved. In other words, predestination. And then there are Bible verses such as "For those whom God foreknew he also predestined" (Romans 8:29).

On the other hand, it might just be that the human perspective is like being at the bottom of a valley and trying to look over into the next valley, while God's perspective is like looking down from above.

Before you freak out thinking God is unfair, consider the possibility that there is good news here. That's what Martin Luther did: "Since God has taken my salvation out of my hands into his, making it depend on his choice and not mine, and has promised to save me,

178

not by my own work or exertion but by his grace and mercy, I am assured and certain both that he is faithful and will not lie to me, and also that he is too great and powerful for any demons or any adversities to be able to break him or to snatch me from him" [LW 33:289].

See also: election; gospel; grace

presence of God \PREH-zihnts-uhv-GAHD\ n. + prep. + n.

The absurd idea that God has *not* wandered off somewhere but is right there with you, even though God is nowhere to be seen.

The Psalms tell us that there is nowhere that we can go, no rock we can hide under, no place so far, no site so black that God cannot find us. Not even under the bed, not in the bathroom with the lights off and the water running—"even there, God's hand will lead us." (That's Psalm 139 if you care to fact-check.)

The fourteen-dollar theological term for this is "immanence," which means that God is everywhere . . . sort of like Starbucks.

P

But even more to the point, there is a special way in which God is especially present with us, and that is in God's name. Where God's name is, there God is. And you, child of God, have that name written all over you; so wherever you go, there God is. Or, as Jesus puts it, "where two or three are gathered in my name, I am there among them" (Matthew 18:20).

So if you're looking around for God, try calling out God's name, and then watch as God comes a-runnin'.

See also: immanence of God; incarnation; omnipresence; absence of God

promise \PRAH-mihs\ n.

A commitment, spoken or written—often viewed with disbelief—that in the future a specified deed will be done (or not done); the only way to receive a promise is to believe it.

"Promises were made to be broken," or so the saying goes. We humans are especially good at making sure that the old saying holds true. God, on the other hand, not only makes promises; God keeps them. Because of the human tendency to break promises, humans often assume that human promises will not be kept.

Promises are one of the main ways that God works. God promises to forgive sins, to bless us, to be with us always, to be our eternal Big Toe (as it were), to give us meaningful work to do in God's kingdom, to give us eternal life on the other side of death, and so on.

And the only way to receive a promise is to believe it. But because all human beings are sinners, we tend not to believe God's promises, assuming, as the song goes, that God is a schmuck like one of us. But God isn't. God keeps promises.

See also: Baptism; Covenant; Jesus; Justification; Predestination

prophet \PRAH-fiht\ n.

The original crazy-talkers—men and women to whom God entrusted an urgent message, causing them to resort to wild stories and wilder behavior in order to get that message across.

Prophets are usually strange. Ask anybody who's met, listened to, or read one, and they'll tell you the same. Prophets are wild-eyed, wild-haired, hell-bent, and strange.

Consider just some of what prophets do. Ezekiel endorses a ridiculously high-fiber diet. (Dudes, he eats a book—Ezekiel 3:1–3—yum; and he's supposed to bake a barley cake over a fire stoked with human dung—Ezekiel 4:9–13—even yummier!) Isaiah treats a boil with a lump of figs (2 Kings 20:7) and names his son Maher-shalal-hash-baz. (Isaiah 8:3—makes Eugene or Dorcas sound good, doesn't it?) And Elisha busts out his prophetic stylings to the sounds of the wheels of steel. (Okay, it was probably a harp—2 Kings 3:11–19.)

See? Prophets are strange, weird, and sometimes nuts. And all of this craziness is part of delivering God's message. It begs the question: Are they nuts because they hear God's Word, or are they likely candidates to receive it because they're nuts? Probably a chicken-and-the-egg thing.

Prophets may be strange, even disturbing, but they serve a very important purpose. Prophets deliver a message from God. Sometimes people think prophets are fortune tellers or future-predictors, but that's not quite right. What they do is speak the WORD OF

GOD—be it threat or promise—and that word pretty much stands. Anybody surprised? It is a thing promised by *God* after all.

If you look at a toddler eating ice cream and say, "Lo, unless this child is bibbed she will, verily, make upon her shirt a wretched mess and cause a doing of laundry. Behold, thus says the experienced parent, thou shalt not serve soft-serve to a small child lest thou incur a messy face and fingers." Does observing this make you a prophet? 'Course not; same thing here. Things happen because God (through the prophet) says they will, not because they are "predicted."

Other people talk about the prophets as social activists. This isn't quite right either. Prophets are concerned with things like JUSTICE and good behavior, but always as they have to do with God's will and God's expectations. That's more like theological activists—bringing God's message to people who need to hear it, even when they might not want to hear it.

So a prophet is someone who delivers messages from God. These messages come to them in different ways: prophets dream dreams, see visions, or hear the Word of God and pass it on by word of mouth or by letter. Or if it were done much today they'd probably come to your email inbox—and probably get caught by the spam filter. So next time you hear the "You've got mail" sound, listen up; it may be one of those strange prophets delivering a message from God.

See also: witness

protestant \PRAH-dih-stuhnt\ adj.

A word meaning "disagreeing," and therefore the perfect word to describe many Christians (including the authors of this book).

Protestant \PRAH-dih-stuhnt\ n.

A Christian belonging to one of many churches that disagreed with the Roman Catholic Church and therefore agreed to form other churches, which in turn disagree with each other.

Generally speaking, religious pilgrimages are not something that Protestant Christians participate in. That's too bad for the city of Speyer, Germany, because it's there that Protestants got their start. In 1526 an imperial convention (back in those days conventions were called "diets"—now that's crazy talk) was held in Speyer. One of the issues that the convention discussed was Europe's growing religious turmoil between the Roman Catholic Church and various other groups who were in disagreement with Rome. The decision was made to let the ruler of every area determine the religious practices in his territory.

However, in 1529, the second "Diet of Speyer" did a big-time one-eighty. The representatives voted to overturn the decision of 1526! The princes who voted in the minority said, "We protest!" In an extremely clever bit of labeling, the protesting princes were dubbed—ta-da!—"protestants."

These days, *Protestant* refers to a wide range of Christian denominations: Lutherans, Presbyterians, Reformed, Baptists, Mennonites,  Covenant, Pentecostals, Seventh-Day Adventists, and many more. Why so many? Because Protestants are not only disagreeable, they like to disagree. Basically almost every time someone disagreed about what they thought was a major issue—a CHURCH dividing issue, as opposed to an *ADIAPHORA* issue— they broke off and started a new church.

Want a simple definition? Try this: Protestants are Christians who reject the authority of the Roman Church and especially of the pope, recognize the Bible as the chief authority in matters of FAITH, and believe that God justifies people by grace through faith, apart from good works.

P

Unlike Roman Catholics, who will refer to themselves as "Catholics," Protestants will rarely say, "I'm a Protestant." Instead, Protestants will say, "I'm a Baptist" or "I'm a Methodist" or "I'm a Lutheran" and so on. Then there are those with-it Christians will tell you simply "I'm a Christian." (Such Christians take to heart the apostle Paul's words to those quarreling Christians in Corinth. Paul reminded those Corinthians that since it was Christ who was crucified, Christ is the only name worth identifying with. Check out 1 Corinthians 1:12–2:2.)

Epilogue: Protestants who go against the grain and make that religious pilgrimage to Speyer will not be disappointed. In 1904 Speyer's Memorial Church was completed. The church—with its 300-foot steeple—commemorates the events surrounding the "Protestation" of 1529. Not surprisingly, Speyer's Roman Catholics did not take the new church as a neighborly gesture. In response, a new Roman Catholic church—with *two* 300-foot steeples—was built a stone's throw away. Only a mean-spirited person would say that the Catholics of Speyer had spire envy.

See also: Catholic; justification; orthodox; Reformation; works, good

providence \PRAH-vih-duhnts\ n.

Every day you are unaware that God is aware of your needs.

Since we each like to think we're pretty awesome, we're not likely to think much about the stuff we have no control over. When is the last time you reflected about how the mix of gases in the atmosphere has to be just right, or we all suffocate? Removing all implications of creationism or intelligent design or whatever, the fact that we have air we can breathe and bodies that work is due to God's providence—God's providing—for us.

It doesn't stop there. Since providence stretches into the things God wants for us in our lives, it also extends to supportive relationships, useful vocations, nurturing church homes, dinner on the table, protection from EVIL, and guidance through the minefields of life. We like to think that we can pull all this stuff off on our own, but the fact remains that without God's constant benevolent intervention, we would probably do what we do best: screw it all up.

Best of all, God does these things whether or not we ask for them—although it doesn't hurt to ask God for specific help when you are aware of your needs. God provides because God can and has promised to do so. We need God, and God comes through for us. It's not that we're *totally* helpless, it's that we're totally *helpless*. Thank heaven that God cares about us.

See also: creature; God; prayer; promise

P

R

rapture \RAP-chuhr\ n.

Now you see it, now you don't—because the teaching is not biblical.

In this not-going-to-happen event, all truly faithful Christians would be beamed from the earth directly to heaven so that they could avoid Satan's seven-year reign before Christ's return at the end of the world. In reality the biblical support for such an event simply does not exist. Kind of like Frankenstein, this monstrous false DOC-TRINE was pieced together from bits of 1 Thessalonians, Matthew, Daniel, and REVELATION—and popularized by a series of pseudo-interpretational novels.

See also: antichrist; eschatology; second coming

redemption \ree-DEHMP-shuhn\ n.

The state resulting from the reinstatement of that which is deemed—being re-deemed.

Redemption is the condition in which the redeemed sinner finds him/herself following the redeeming activity of the Redeemer.

The action that leads to the redemption of the sinner is much like that which leads to the recycling of cans and bottles for $ .05 in VT, ML, NY, IA, MA, OR, or CT; except the recycled material is not tin or glass but a whole person, the recycled is saved not from the trash heap but from SIN and DEATH (Romans 3:22), and the exchange is not in money but the blood of Christ – the Redeemer.

See also: Atonement; Justification; Salvation

Reformation \reh-fuhr-MĀ-shuhn\ n.

A revolution within Christianity that started in 1517 and is still happening, needs to happen again, or needs to stop happening, depending on whom you talk to.

The story goes like this. On Halloween of 1517, in a little German village, a kid dressed up as a monk went trick-or-treating at the local church. The kid was given some yummy indulgences. But he didn't like indulgences, so he protested, thereby starting the Reformation of the Christian church.

R

We kid about the kid. Here's how the Reformation really went down. On October 31, 1517, in Wittenberg, Germany, a thirty-four-year-old professor who lived in the local monastery offered ninety-five theses for debate. The professor reportedly posted the theses on the door of a local church. (No, not feces. Ha ha. Don't think that you are the first to think of that joke.)

Anyway, the professor's name was Dr. Martin Luther King Jr. Oops. Make that Martin Luther. The two names do get confused now and then. Although in fact the great U.S. civil rights leader is indeed named in honor of the great German reformer. And no, we're not kidding this time. Look it up!

Anyway the pages of the theses from the Wittenberg door were published, and they sold like hotcakes across Europe. That anything published could sell like hotcakes was amazing in itself, since hotcakes don't sell that well anymore. But thanks to the then-recent invention of the printing press (an early form of the internet), pamphlets and books could be printed inexpensively and quickly. Luther's famous *Ninety-five Theses* hit Europe like a tabloid headline: "Pope Wrong?! Seven-headed Monk Challenges 1,000 Years of Church Teaching!!" You think we're exaggerating, but one of Luther's opponents actually did publish a cartoon depicting Luther as a monster with seven heads.

R

Back to the story. Luther kept on reading the Bible and kept on calling for church reform. As the "Luther problem" grew, Luther was brought before the gathered might of the Holy Roman Empire and asked to renounce his teachings. But he refused, saying that going against the Bible "was neither right nor safe." He was kicked out of the church (aka "excommunicated") but continued to teach and write and inspire and organize.

Luther's here-I-stand-up-to-da-man moment is often remembered as one of the great events in Western history, a victory for the "little guy" against a much stronger opponent—like David and Goliath or the Battle of Thermopylae (Sparta!). But Luther's original intent was more modest. He merely wanted to reform the church, not start a new one. And yet the cat was out of the bag. If Luther could say that his own reading of the Bible was correct, then others could say the same. And so they did. Ulrich Zwingli, Thomas Müntzer, John Calvin—even Henry VIII—are just some of the other reformers who differed with Rome *and* with Luther *and* with each other.

The result? Well, today there are Roman Catholics and Lutherans, Anglicans and Presbyterians, Methodists and Mennonites, Baptists and Pentecostals, evangelicals and "non-denominationals," and more. A whole smorgasbord of churches. Five-hundred million Protestants subdivided into more than thirty thousand independently operating groups! (Real Statistics™).

The Western church has divided and subdivided over essential issues, such as faith and good works, and less-essential issues, such as marriage, ordination, worship, baptism, communion, language, and coffee. Okay, maybe not coffee. But we wouldn't be surprised.

So is the Reformation over? Should it be? Or do we need another one, where change means more cooperation and less division? Today, the number of Christians is on the decline in the global north but increasing in the global south. What's up with that?

There's an old slogan: *ecclesia semper reformanda*—"the church is always reforming." What is the church of the future going to look like? God only knows (literally). But you can trust that whatever it looks like, it will be filled with salt and light.

See also: adiaphora; catholic; church; ecclesiology; indulgence; pastor/priest; Protestant

religion \ree-lih-juhn\ n.

A system of beliefs and practices that are meant to nourish a life of faith, hope, and love, but often cause deep skepticism and despair, and drive people away from God.

Religion sometimes gets a bad rap. Karl Marx famously remarked that "religion is the opium of the people." Mr. Wednesday (in Neil Gaiman's *American Gods*) quipped that opium has become the religion of the masses. So take that, Karl.

Of course, sometimes religion deserves its bad rap when it falls on its face or fails to show up when, where, and how it's needed. There is actually more to Marx's quote about religion that gets at these needs; he said, "Religion is the sigh of the oppressed creature, the heart of a heartless world, and the soul of soulless conditions." Better, but still not quite there, because that's only part of what religion is. Religion also ought to be the response to the oppressed creature's sigh. Right religion—true religion, religion at its best—is all of this. Without the opium.

The book of James puts it this way: "Religion that is pure and undefiled before God, the Father, is this: to care for orphans and widows in their distress, and to keep oneself unstained by the world" (James 1:27). That last part is pretty tough. If you're anything like us, you've got "world" stains all over you, and not just a little bit either; we're talkin' grass stains on blue jeans, beet juice on a white polo, oil on your garage floor kind of staining. Hard to get out. But the first part? We can totally do that. We can care for orphans, widows, and any sighing creature.

As flawed, prone to silliness, and downright human as religion can be, it's what we've got. Some might say that religion must be true because only God could work through something so crazy. Kind of like the cross. But religion that stands in the way of a genuine faith—of life-giving hope, of heartfelt love—is no good. Religion ought to serve these things, not rule them or obscure them. And true religion does just this: it serves.

R See also: church; service; tradition

remnant \REHM-**nehnt**\ n.

The leftover, unusable scrap of material from which the Divine Quilter can sew a quilt.

Psalm 139 says God is both a knitter (v. 13) and a weaver (v. 15). But we like to think of God as a quilter. When the world says, "Ew, toss it," God says, "No, wait!" and compulsively holds onto tiny scraps and bits of old, ratty stuff. God takes that ratty stuff (the metaphor is that we are the ratty stuff, by the way) and stitches it into a gorgeous quilt, enters it in the fair, and totally gets the Best In Show prize (the metaphor is that we are also the best stuff, by the way).

The Bible testifies that God does the best work with remnants. In Genesis, Joseph and his fancy coat got ripped down to remnants, beaten up, and sold into slavery by his brothers. But once he landed in Egypt, God stuck with him, and Joseph rose to serve in Pharaoh's court. (He used an old, wooden racquet.) But when famine threatened to starve his older brothers, God used Joseph to save the whole family: "God sent me before you to preserve for you a remnant on earth, and to keep alive for you many survivors" (Genesis 45:7). God doesn't just use those scraps to look good—God uses them to find and save more scraps. Basically, God hoards salvifically.

R

God continues this quilting pattern, over and over, to save the day. In the days of Elijah, the oppressive King Ahab had persecuted God's people almost out of existence. But God used Elijah and a remnant of only seven thousand faithful to preserve the nation (1 Kings 19). When Babylon conquered Judah, destroying the temple and razing

Jerusalem, a remnant went into exile in Babylon. There they stayed faithful to God. And God sustained the people.

Thus it has been over and over throughout history. At times, only a remnant remains. But do you know what? Some of God's best work starts with a few scraps of cloth. So go talk to that scrappy quilter, and tell her, "Do you know what? I think I can learn a lot about God from you."

See also: creation; faithfulness; exile

repentance \ree-PEHN-tuhnts\ n.

The change in a person's behavior that follows recognition of having sinned and immediately precedes further sinning.

Repentance (or repent; or repent-ing, -ed, or -er; or repentalization) usually describes a life-changing about-face, most effectively encouraged by cardboard signs held on street-corners or adorning the front of soapboxes. Most people are more comfortable with the abstract noun than with the verbal form, especially when applied to others.

R

As egg-headed Bible types will tell you, *repentance* is a translation of a couple different words. There is the Greek word *metanoia*, which means "change your mind," and the Hebrew word *shub*, which means to "turn around" or "return." The English word *repentance* (or repentitude or repentifer or repentification) is used to translate *both* of those words. So the next time you hear a preacher or Bible scholar making a big deal out of translation, we suggest two options. (1) Doodle in your bulletin and wait for her to get to the point.

(2) Wait until Q & A or after worship and ask him if the word in question is a verbal form that has been nominalized, vice versa, or if it is a cognate that may or may not have a one-to-one functional correspondence. Then watch the wanna-be-wordsmith squirm. Unless of course it's one of the present authors; then you should just listen and be amazed.

Repentance is an important feature in the Bible: it is core to the preaching of Jesus, Peter, and Paul (see Mark 1:15; Acts 3:38; 13; 19); it is what Hebrews calls the "basic teaching" about Christ and the "foundation" of what the church does (Hebrews 6:1); and it is, according to the ANGEL Gabriel in the movie *Constantine* (Did you see it? It was beautiful), humankind's singular gift from God. The recurring pattern in the Bible is one of humanity's failings and failures taking over and taking the place that God ought to have in a person's life—and God's calling to them to return.

There are, of course, many things one may need to repent of—simple sins, unbelief or rejection of the gospel, the intents of one's heart, or chronic nose-picking. The Bible—Old and New Testament alike—urges repentance and promises FORGIVENESS. Repentance is not, however, merely rote or mechanical. John the Baptist calls for a repentance that bears "worthy fruit." (It's with the whole "brood of vipers" thing; John rocked.) There is then some expectation that repentance ought not be simply cosmetic or convenient but rather lead to renewed efforts at walking in God's will and way.

So repentance, if taken seriously, will become a habit, a way of life. As a pastor once put it a long time ago, "The entire life of the believer should be one of repentance."

Other ways of referring to the act of repentance may include but need not be limited to backpedaling from sin, running way from bad habits, tactical withdrawal from being a morally deficient moron, and the un-hardening of one's heart.

See also: absolution; born again; confession; confessional; contrition; forgiveness

resurrection \reh-zuh-REHK-shuhn\ n.

To be raised imperishable; to get stamped "best by ∞."

Ever had expired mayonnaise? Ever bit into a Twinkie the day *after* the packaging says it's no good? Well, wouldn't it be great if the mayo never went bad? If the seal of freshness on that Twinkie never let death's bony fingers steal that delicious, creamy-filling-ed, golden sponge cake's goodness? Alas, all things come to an end. As Benjamin Franklin remarked, "Nothing can be said to be certain, except death and taxes." And we might add expiration dates to that.

But wait a minute—slow your roll. Not so fast. Hold those horses, Skippy. Listen to what Paul says about death, baptism, and resurrection: "Do you not know that all of us who have been baptized into Christ Jesus were baptized into his death? Therefore, we have been buried with him by baptism into death, so that, just as Christ was raised from the dead by the glory of the Father, so we too might walk in newness of life" (Romans 6:3–4). And, "Christ has been raised from the dead, the first fruits of those who have died. For since death came through a human being, the resurrection of the dead has also come through a human being; for as all die in Adam, so all will be made alive in Christ" (1 Corinthians 15:20–22).

The point is that God has promised to undo the expiration date, to roll it back, and raise us up. If he was the first fruits of the dead, then we get to be the next fruits. Just as Christ was raised from the dead, we will be too. Game over? For death, maybe. For all who believe in Jesus, it's game on.

But resurrection is about more than the life we are promised after death; resurrection is about the life we get to live now too. Here's one more from Paul: "Listen, I will tell you a mystery! We will not all die, but we will all be changed, in a moment, in the twinkling of an eye, at the last trumpet. For the trumpet will sound, and the dead will be raised imperishable, and we will be changed. For this perishable body must put on imperishability, and this mortal body must put on immortality" (1 Corinthians 15:51–53).

Finally, we are being resurrected every single day. In a very real way, we die in our sins daily. Our lives are dead and worthless through our constant sin and rebellion. However, in the act of continual forgiveness granted to us through God's grace, we are reborn as new, forgiven, and resurrected humans. This is an actual resurrection. Our sins kill us, but God's forgiveness makes us alive again. And again. And again.

Apparently, it's only taxes that are certain. Sorry, Ben.

See also: baptism; death; heaven; hell; judgment; sin

revelation \reh-vuh-LĀ-shuhn\ n.

Reason's embarrassing brother-in-law, who married into the family and is often the source of awkward pauses at the dinner table, but who expresses things nobody else can.

You know him: Uncle Skip, who seems to have a satellite link to some strange databases and offers startling advice at the Thanksgiving table. He makes your normally placid Aunt Martha retreat to the kitchen to scour pots and causes your dad to laugh until milk comes out of his nose. Bizarre as the mojo he brings and the wake he leaves is, he's family.

The Christian family might make more sense or be more organized without it, but the Christian family just wouldn't be the same without revelation—God's will and Word communicated to us. God communicates with us in ways that cannot be proven, only believed. This is a central matter for Christian faith; deal with it.

R

God actually loves the world and is so committed to the fabric of CREATION and the way things work that God communicates through the things of the world. Jesus is the fullest picture of who God is. The BIBLE is God's Word in ink on paper. Pastors, prophets, and apostles are God's Word spoken and shared by human beings.

Of course, we don't check our brains at the baptismal font. God's love for the world includes reason, intellect, and human judgment. FAITH in revelation comes with permission to be skeptical of special and direct revelations, secret knowledge, and anyone who claims full ownership of the whole truth . . . and of Uncle Skip.

See also: apostle; Bible; pastor/priest; prophet

righteous \RI-chuhs\ adj.

Everything that you are not but that God wants you to be.

In *Finding Nemo*, when the surfing turtle Crash catches a ride on the eastern Australian current, he ecstatifies, "Righteous! Righteous!"

And that pretty much sums it up. To be righteous is to be spot on in everything God would have you be spot on about.

In the Bible a righteous scale measures accurately, a righteous promisor keeps her promises, a righteous daughter cares for her parents, and a righteous brother sings unchained melodies melodiously.

The bad news: God wants you to be righteous. The good news: God *is* righteous.

R

See also: righteousness

righteousness \RI-chuhs-nihs\ n.

An attribute of God that we like when we imagine we have something coming to us that we want, but one we don't like when we remember we have other things coming to us that we don't want.

Imagine that you have just been horribly wronged in some monstrous but non–life-threatening way—probably by your little brother, but let's not name names here. *Who would you go to?*

Now imagine that you have just horribly wronged someone else—yes, we know, you're a good little angel, but just use your imagination—we're just pretending. *Who would you be afraid the person you had wronged would go to (the sniveling little tattletale)?*

The person or persons one runs to when wronged are people who display the quality of *righteousness*, that is, a quality of making just decisions and offering fair solutions to problems. With us, it was our mothers. And woe to the little tattler who runs to mommy with a lie!

R

In terms of perfect righteousness, only God has it. And here is the crazy thing—you might think that God's perfect righteousness might lead God to condemn and punish all of us since, well, we have all wronged someone at some time. If so, you would be surprised. Through Jesus, God has promised to be faithful to you. And God's righteousness means that God will keep that promise—no matter how much you screw up.

Oh, by the way, God still wants you to try to be like your mother—you can't do it, but try to be as righteous as you can. Your neighbor will appreciate it.

See also: attributes of God; justice; promise; righteous

R

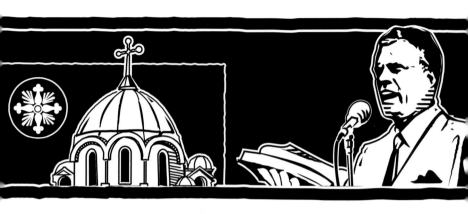

S

Sabbath \sa-bihth\ n.

A special day for rest and worship, which we think we don't need—even though God did and does.

"Remember the Sabbath and keep it holy." *Sabbath* comes from the Hebrew verb *shabbat*, which means "to cease." As a productive civilization proud of its work ethic, we're not very good at "ceasing." In fact, we're downright pathetic at it. We work 'round the clock. Worse, we expect others to work 'round the clock for us (forgetting that the original commandment gave servants and animals a day of rest—in other words, it was the first "labor law").

Yet God built a rhythm into the very fabric of CREATION—six days of work and one day of ceasing work. The earth itself requires a Sabbath. In ancient times every seventh year was a Sabbath year for the

202

land to lie fallow. So you'd think that if the very soil we live upon needs a Sabbath, we who work (upon) the soil would figure it out. But noooo.

And we need Sabbath for WORSHIP—so that God can work new life in us rather than just us working ourselves to death. Sabbath is both a time for rest and when God can work things like FORGIVENESS, renewal, and HOPE through the Word and sacraments.

Maybe "remember the Sabbath" is being too polite about it. There's no "Thou shalt" or "Thou shalt not." Perhaps a re-wording is in order. Something like, "Hey, Morons! What is wrong with you people!? 168 hours in a week is not enough for you? I ask you to set aside just one day so that you can rest up long enough to be renewed for the coming week, and what do you do? Double overtime, eighty-hour work weeks, and Super Centers open 24/7! How are you ever going to slow down long enough  so that you can gather together in Christian worship, so that you can sit still long enough to hear the Word that I have to share with you? *Stop! Listen!*"

See also: means of grace; sacrament; sermon; Word of God; worship

S

sacrament \sa-kruh-mihnt\ n.

Not to be confused with Alpha-Bits, sacraments are visible words that you can eat, drink, and be bathed in.

One day Duh asked his pastor about the sacraments. She has a lot of patience, which you need to have to be a pastor, especially Duh's pastor. (If you haven't met Duh yet, we suggest you take a quick look at the entry on GOD.)

Duh: Pastor, I've been struggling with chronic halitosis and other forms of bad breath. My dentist suggested some breath freshener. But my wife said my breath needs divine intervention, so can you give me some sacramints?

Pastor: Duh, we all need divine intervention, but I think you mean *sacraments*—BAPTISM and COMMUNION. They won't help with your breath, but they will help your faith life.

Duh: What is a sacraments?

Pastor: What *are* the sacraments. The best way to understand the sacraments is to think of them as visible words. They are the way that God says, "I love you." God says this to us in bread, wine, and water—the simplest things of everyday life.

Duh: Visible words? Like in the Paul Bunyan story where it was so cold one winter that all of the lumberjacks' words froze in the air? And then when the spring thaw came, the words were zipping around at high speed, taking out the lumberjacks right and left?

Pastor: Wow, Duh, I'm speechless.

Duh: How many sacraments are there?

Pastor: Different Christian groups have different numbers of sacraments, depending on how they define what a sacrament is. We say that to be a sacrament, a ritual must have been commanded by Christ, include an earthly sign, and be a MEANS OF GRACE. So we have two sacraments: baptism, in which the sign is water, and communion, in which the earthly signs of bread and wine carry God's words, "This is my body, this is my blood."

Duh: So the pastor changes the bread into Christ's body and the wine into Christ's blood! I get it! I get it!

Pastor: Uh, not so fast, my friend. The pastor doesn't change the bread, wine, or water into anything. Pastors don't have special powers. The bread, wine, and water remain simple ol' bread, wine, and water. But the WORD OF GOD is spoken with them, and thus they are visible words—they truly are the body and blood of Christ for sinners.

Duh: For sinners? Don't I have to earn the right to receive the sacraments?

Pastor: No. The whole point of a sacrament is that they offer us God's grace. And grace is for sinners, not perfect people. It says in the Bible, "While we were still sinners Christ died for us" (Romans 5:8). There is no requirement to receive a sacrament except that you know you are a sinner and need grace.

Duh: Hey, then I qualify!

Pastor: Yep, and so do I.

See also: grace; justification; works, good

sacrifice \sa-krih-fis\ v.

To forfeit something either for one's own benefit or for the benefit of another (one who is usually oblivious to his or her need—and thus needs it all the more).

The chicken's eggs are sacrificed for your baking, her feathers for your comfort, and her whole body for your dinner. Bad for the chicken, good for you.

Jesus sacrifices his power for your sins, his equality with God for your humanity, and himself for your SALVATION. Good for you, and in the end, not bad for Jesus, whom God raised from the dead. In the case of Christ, the sacrifice is a gift not to God but from God to you and on your behalf.

In Christian theology, the only Sacrifice with a capital S is Jesus. But some people make smaller sacrifices—money, time, food, dental floss—as a response to the Sacrifice that Jesus made. These smaller sacrifices are for the benefit of your NEIGHBOR (not yourself).

See also: atonement; happy exchange; justification; redemption

saint \sānt\ n.

Every Christian, including you, and many other persons with whom you wouldn't want out to hang (as Winston Churchill might have said).

So you think you already know what a saint is? Let's guess: someone (a) who is so admirable that if you died, you'd want them to take care of your puppy but (b) with whom you wouldn't want to go to an R-rated movie. And you certainly wouldn't want to be one! As a T-shirt we saw on a little kid said, "I tried being good, but I got bored."

In this view, saints are people like Mother Theresa who are so selfless that we feel downright wicked by comparison. But in the New Testament, the word *saint* never refers to a special class of super-duper-Christian; rather it always refers to all Christians. For instance, the letter to the Ephesians is addressed "to the saints in Ephesus." Saints are not saintly because of what they do but because of what Christ has done for them. Christian saints

are identified not by their own wisdom, good works, HOLINESS, or wholeness but by the fact that they belong to Jesus.

And that means, of course, that you are qualified to be a saint, too. As is your worst nightmare of a NEIGHBOR. Groucho Marx may have said, "I don't want to be a member of any club that will accept me as a member," but Jesus said, in effect, "Only sinners need apply—and I will make you saints."

See also: church; sanctification; simultaneously saint and sinner

salvation \sal-vĀ-shuhn\ n.

Rescue by God from something bad and for something good, which we deny to enemies on principle, promise to friends as a reward, and assume is our personal right.

In the theme park ride that is the Christian life, debate rages about the timing of salvation—whether it's at the point of acquiring a ticket (BAPTISM), the moment you board the log ride (begin to take your FAITH seriously), the high spot at which you hurl (realize you are scared and need rescue), the point at which you raise your hands reflexively into the air (start to love God), or the comedown as you pass through the exit turnstile (enter into eternal life). People celebrate various moments. And wobbly-headed philosophers first have to define what a "moment" is. (No, we are not kidding; we have sat through lectures about this sort of ludicrosity.) Most agree, however, that human salvation is *from* something bad, *for* something good, and accomplished by God.

From something bad: "Save me, O God, for the waters have come up to my neck!" (Psalm 69:1). Psalmists, Christians, Israelites, disciples, recovering addicts, and survivors of all kinds testify that God saved them *from something*—illness, addiction, enemies, death, natural disasters, poverty, despair, and above all, *from ourselves*. This puts a helpful reality to a term that can easily become abstract and theoretical. God's salvation is for real people in real circumstances and situations. In the big picture, salvation is from SIN and its consequences. But this takes concrete form in the world—death being the singularly unpleasant elephant in everyone's room, present not only at check-out time but wherever and whenever fear and anxiety creep in and seem like the final word.

For something good: "I will redeem you with an outstretched arm and with mighty acts of judgment. I will take you as my people, and I will be your God. You shall know that I am the Lord your God" (Exodus 6:6b–7a). Saved from DEATH, it follows that what God intends by all these rescue operations is life. This life should not be mistaken as just scraping by but a joyful, abundant *vitality*. God saves us in order to have a relationship with us. God and the saved people belong to one another, are reconciled, and in love. This redeemed life is more than survival. It entails a freedom from fear and despair, freedom to live in and enjoy the CREATION, and freedom for generous SERVICE to and love for one's NEIGHBOR.

Accomplished by God: "For not in my bow do I trust, nor can my sword save me" (Psalm 44:6). The ingenuity and resourcefulness of people seems to know no bounds. Origami. The Chia Pet. Ice makers. In the end, though, even our brilliance can't save us from death or really free us for life. Salvation belongs to and is accomplished by God alone, in Jesus Christ, for the sake of God's LOVE. It is the process and state of having been rescued from everything we love—and love to hate—about ourselves.

See also: atonement; forgiveness; grace; justification; soteriology; wrath of God

sanctification \sānk-tih-fih-kā-shuhn\ n.

The process by which a confessed sinner becomes holier than thou.

As with education, *sanctification* describes a process that transforms a person or thing from one state to another. In this case, the goal is HOLINESS. The big conundrum is this: How do you make a sinner into a SAINT? (Insert warning sound here—*ah-ooo-gah!!*—this is a trick question.)

It is clear from the Bible that sanctification is about holiness and related to the act of JUSTIFICATION or salvation accomplished by Jesus. Some suggest that it's a slow and painful process, like junior high or getting braces on your teeth. At some point the believer's spiritual complexion clears up, and his or her spiritual bite achieves proper alignment. As this argument goes, sanctification is progressive, a combination of inspiration and perspiration, and it results in a Christlike glow that must be guarded like that sofa in your grandparents' living room (the one with the plastic slipcover that nobody ever got to sit on).

If you've been reading this book, you'll see the problem we have with this "keep off the grass" version of sanctification: it turns sanctification into something you have to do for yourself. *You* don't make a sinner into a saint, the HOLY SPIRIT does: "God chose you as the first fruits for salvation through *sanctification by the Holy Spirit*" (2 Thessalonians 2:13; emphasis added). Jesus justifies us; sanctification is the work the Spirit does in our life after justification. It's like the best two-for-one deal imaginable. Don't go looking for that rosy glow, though, because it's

no sure sign of anything. We're saved and holy not because of our complexion or our dazzling smile—we remain sinners even after we are saved. Our role in sanctification is getting used to living as both sinner and saint.

See also: grace; salvation; simultaneously saint and sinner

Satan \sā-tihn\ n.

The multinational corporate head of evil; aka the devil, father of lies, Lucifer, fallen angel, the tempter, the prince of darkness.

To paraphrase Forrest Gump, EVIL is as evil does. Some Christians do not believe in a literal devil, believing that the concept of a devil is a convenient excuse that we cite in order to justify our own short-comings. Others believe that evil has a corporate head, who is a fallen ANGEL (Luke 10:18), tempted Jesus (Luke 4:1–13), and makes promises but never keeps them. Know this: the devil, if there be one, has no power over you. Jesus Christ has claimed you, and nothing can separate you from his love (see Romans 8:31–39).

See also: fall, the

second coming \SEH-kuhnd-KUH-meeng\ n.

Just as with Jesus's first coming to earth, an event in which we can expect Jesus to confound all our expectations—to our eternal joy and gratitude.

Like kids riding in the back seat on a family vacation, the disciples wanted to know "when." How long until this happens, Jesus? The Lord, like a parent who had heard the question one too many times, responded, "But about that day or hour no one knows, neither the angels in heaven, nor the Son, but only the Father" (Mark 13:32). And so . . .

. . . ever since, people have tried to predict when Christ will come again. What are these people, stupid? Don't answer that, we already know the answer.

As the Left Behind series of books has shown, imagining Jesus's return and the suffering, conflict, trial, tribulation, rapture, and judgment we would like to see are fodder for a bestseller. Make that a *fiction* best-seller. But Christ says only this: "Keep alert, for you do not know when the time will come" (Mark 13:33).

Although the Left Behind books want to make the second coming a dark and scary thing, it is really good news. The second coming is the PROMISE that the future of all CREATION is in God's hands, so we don't have to worry about it. And so, we do.

See also: heaven; judgment; rapture

sermon \SUHR-muhn\ n.

A series of mono-, bi-, and polysyllabic sounds that (1) made more sense the night before, (2) can bore to death, and (3) can raise the dead to new life.

Not to be confused with drunken ramblings, many sermons are completed long after the sun goes down on Saturday—about the time that bars close. Often written and always spoken, a sermon is a preaching event—it *does* something. Because some human preacher speaks a sermon with a human tongue, sermons can bore to death. Because the HOLY SPIRIT speaks the word into the hearer's ear, sermons can raise the dead to new life. True sermons are not a human's opinion; they open the biblical story and the ears of listeners to the actual WORD OF GOD.

See also: faith; means of grace; pastor/priest

S

service \SUHR-vihs\ n.

Many things to many people.

In electricity, service means that something is supplied, connected. In economics, service is a non-material good that can be exchanged for money or for another service. In lips, service is what you said to your mom that got you your mouth washed out with soap. In theology, service is what you do for others because of what God has done for you. It is not required for SALVATION. It's one way we respond after being saved. Service calls us beyond ourselves to recognize and actually do something to meet the needs of another.

See also: ethics; neighbor; vocation

silence of God \sī-lihnts-uhv-GAHD\ n. + prep. + n.

The "still small voice" that is, apparently, so still and so small that you still can't hear it.

Maybe God's voice is a "high pitched voice" that is so high and so pitched that only dogs can hear it. Okay, maybe not.

Have you ever considered that if prayer is talking to God, and thanksgiving is talking to God, and praise is . . . um . . . talking to

CRAZY TALK

God, it would appear that we do a lot of talking to God? But does God talk back? Does God answer? Does God say, "You're welcome" (which, after all, is just good manners!)? Does God tell us, "Stop, you're embarrassing me!"? Or not?

It seems that God used to talk, and quite a lot. According to the book of Genesis, creation was all God talking, one six-day soliloquy. And God didn't just talk to God's self either; God spoke to Adam and Eve, Abraham, and Moses. God spoke to Saul, David, Isaiah, and all those other prophets. God spoke quite a lot.

So how about now? When we are enduring those long, dark hours of the soul, will God speak to us? God already has. In the book of Hebrews we can hear this great, good news: "Long ago God spoke to our ancestors in many and various ways by the prophets, but in these last days he has spoken to us by a Son" (Hebrews 1:1–2).

God has spoken to us in Jesus—in his teaching, in his story, in his death and resurrection.

Despite the rumors, God isn't dead. Or mute. Or, like a child or an angry spouse, controlling the argument by not talking. But it sure can feel that way sometimes. And that's when we can take a cue from the prophet Elijah, who heard God in the sheer silence (check out 1 Kings 19:11–13). God is there in the silence. Let the one who has ears, hear!

See also: Bible; Christ (Messiah); gospel; Word of God; presence of God; theodicy

simultaneously saint and sinner \si-muhl-ᴛᴀ̄ɴ-ee-uhs-lee-sᴀ̄ɴᴛ-and-sɪʜ-nuhr\ adj.

Being at one and the same time who you think you are and who you really are.

This term is more fun in Latin: *simul iustis et peccator.* These wacky Latin words explain why a good Christian like you can really want to be nicer to your stupid coworker—maybe even pull it off for a week or two—but eventually crack him upside the head anyway. The term effectively means that even though God has made you holy by saving you from yourself, you are still yourself—and thus you fully still suck.

Now some people think that once you become Christian, you are changed—like a caterpillar metamorphosing into a butterfly. Such people think that Christians are essentially different once they experience God's ɢʀᴀᴄᴇ—like Spiderman after the bite. But look in the mirror. Do you see any wings, either of a butterfly or an ᴀɴɢᴇʟ? Nope, we don't either.

Paul wrote in Romans 7 that no matter how much he wants it, he can't do good stuff; conversely, no matter how much he hates being a jerk, he still is. Paul knows that in spite of the good the Spirit can do through him, he's still a slave to sɪɴ just like all of us. That goes for all Christians.

And yet, all Christians are simultaneously saints because God has established a relationship with the sinner. That is what's different about a Christian—the relationship that God initiates with us. It

216

means we can admit we are sinners. It means that we can try to love our NEIGHBOR. And it means that God considers us holy saints, even though we are still sinners, too.

See also: church; holy & holiness

sin \sihn\ n.

(1) Why people suck. (2) How people suck.

You might have noticed how a great many people have a hard time getting along. This goes for individual guys and gals as well as neighborhoods, churches, corporations, governments, mobs, and families. Sometimes this non-niceness comes out as overt gun-knife-or-missile-toting physical violence or waspish verbal and emotional aggression. Sometimes it comes across as dead-eyed indifference, crass cynicism, or even deer-in-the-headlights paralysis. However attired, what's at work in the background is a universal human condition known variously as self-centeredness, ego, and other more or less clinical, casual, or caustic terms. In short: we suck. Read the newspaper. Study history. Listen to yourself when you drive. Admit it.

Theologically, people suck at being human the way God intends humans to be because of a condition known as *sin*. Also known as "fallenness," "brokenness," and "the human condition," *sin* refers to the state of who we are and the condition we are stuck in. The biblical story goes like this: God created everything and it was good (Genesis 1); God created human beings to play a special role within creation (Genesis 1–2); sin entered into the world due to the rebellion

S

of the first human beings (Genesis 3); ever since then, God worked to cure the disease of sin (see the entire rest of the Bible).

The condition of sin has many unfortunate side effects. Instead of trusting and taking God at God's word, we place our trust in other gods—most often the one who wears our face and clothes. Instead of trusting our neighbors, we distrust them and drive them away.

The word *sin* is also used to describe the individual moments in which we all go about our sucking. Because of sin (the condition of sucking), we sin (we do things that suck). We commit individual sins in thousands of ways every day.

Egg-headed ethicists divide sins into two different types—sins of commission and sins of omission. A sin of commission might sound like sin for which you get a 10 percent payout, but actually this is something you do that you are not supposed to do. You may recall that some commandments are "*not*" commandments—do not steal, do not kill, do not pick your nose, and so on. When you do something that you are *not* supposed to do, this is a sin of commission. There are also sins of omission, which you have probably already figured out are things that you are supposed to do but fail to—like loving your NEIGHBOR, loving God, and chewing with your mouth closed.

It should be noted that although sin is a "people" thing, the rest of CREATION is also fallen and suffers from the condition of sin—natural disasters, accidents, and the like are signs that nature, too, is fallen.

An effective remedy for sin will not focus on the symptoms (the individual sins) but the source (the condition of sin). This is why Jesus had to die for us.

See also: Decalogue; fall, the; forgiveness; justification; law; law, uses of the

sojourner \soH-juhrn-uhr\ n. (aka immigrant)

One with no place, no space, no race—who can't stay here, but can't go home (yet).

It's the existential ennui of many a college student: your family doesn't feel like family any more, but the dorm is not your home. It's the saccharine plot of many a Hollywood tear-jerker: the one you love is not who you thought they were, and now you're cut adrift. It's the melancholy plight of many a last call: you don't have to go home, but you can't stay here. Hollywood movies may elevate the role of the drifter, the lone knight, or the last cowboy, but we all recognize the loss in not having a place to really, truly belong.

In the Old Testament, your place was in one spot: your family. Your extended family was everything—your employer, your school, your health plan, your retirement plan, your criminal justice system . . . everything. Just imagine holiday dinners—every dinner would be a combination of quarterly work-performance reviews, final exams, dental exams, and the traditional airing of the grievances (copyright *Seinfeld*). While this social arrangement could be more awkward than your mom's dance moves, there was one big upside: someone in

S

the family would always be there to help you out. There was Uncle Gary, who could fix anything. And Cousin Mike, who would get you out of a legal jam. And Aunt Cari, who could solve any social problem.

But if you got separated from your family system in Old Testament times, or your family system died out, you were a sojourner. Unlike our society's John Wayne wannabes, there's no glamor in being a sojourner. It's lonely and dangerous. Joseph was a sojourner in Egypt (Genesis 37–50). Ruth was a sojourner in Bethlehem (Ruth 1–4). Mary, Joseph, and baby Jesus were sojourners in Bethlehem and later in Egypt (Matthew 1).

If you got in trouble, to whom could you turn? Where would you go when you were but halfway there and livin' on a prayer? Take God's hand; you'll make it, we swear. (We just gave you an ear-worm, didn't we? You'll be singing or hearing "Living on a Prayer" all day, won't you? Sorry. Okay, not really. "Oooooo-ooooo, we're half way there . . . ")

The message of the Bible is that we are all sojourners in this life, whether we are surrounded by unbearable cousins and siblings or completely alone. When we find trouble or trouble finds us, reach up and reach out—for God. And at the end of life's road, there is an eternal home with an eternal Father who has promised to welcome everyone home.

But for now, if you need something fixed, then call Uncle Gary.

See also: pilgrimage; prayer; salvation

Son of God \SUHN-uhv-GAHD\ n.

The title for Jesus he hardly ever used for himself and, accordingly, got him killed.

Have you ever said the following? "I believe in Jesus Christ, God's only Son our Lord." Son of God—that's one of the things Christians call Jesus.

Jesus gets called lots of things—Lord, rabbi, king of the Jews, awesome (never did like that song), cute (what, you don't think Mary thought he was cute, all swaddled in a manger?)—but none of these names or titles seems to have caused as much of a stir as "Son of God." Of all the times this exact phrase gets used in the Bible, only twice does Jesus use it himself. It's striking that this controversial title is so often given to Jesus by others. And the list of those others is crazy:

- The Devil when he tries to tempt him (Matthew 4:3, 6)
- The demon-possessed who recognize him (Matthew 8:29; Mark 3:11; Luke 8:28)
- The mockers who mock him on the cross (Matthew 24:40)
- The disciples when he stills the storm (Matthew 14:33)

A motley crew of folks calling Jesus the Son of God. But there's more. One of the most consistent uses of this title is by those who are confessing their faith in Jesus.

- Peter (Matthew 16:16)
- John (John 1:34)

221

- Nathanael (John 1:49)
- Martha (John 11:27)
- Paul (Acts 9:20)

So what is at stake? Why is Jesus killed because he claimed to be the Son of God (John 19:7)? Why do those who follow him call him Son of God? The answer to both questions is the same: because to call Jesus "Son of God" means to claim that God was present and at work in Jesus Christ in a unique way, in a way totally different than the way God has been present or at work in any other person in history.

The Bible puts it this way: "In Christ God was reconciling the world to himself" (2 Corinthians 5:19a). That is a drop-your-jaw-and-wipe-the-drool-off-your-chin sort of claim! Jesus Christ was not just another all-around good guy or wise teacher. Jesus was the presence and activity of God, through which God reconciled the world to himself!

And there is more. Because Jesus is the Son of God, you too are a child of God. Because Jesus is the Son of God, we have become his brothers and sisters (check out Matthew 12:49 and John 19:26). And it means that if you believe that Jesus is the Son of God, you will "conquer the world" (1 John 5:5).

So have you said it lately? Try it with us now: "I believe in Jesus Christ, God's only Son our Lord." Ah. How good does that feel?

See also: Christ (Messiah); incarnation; Jesus; Trinity

soteriology \soh-tih-ree-ah-luh-jee\ n.

The often disposable theories about who is worth saving and how they are saved.

Soter means "savior" in Greek, making the word effectively *saviorology*. We think this sounds much cooler since it states the straightforward intent of the word: the study of the way your sinful self gets saved. Ideally, it would be easy enough to say that Jesus's death and resurrection conquers DEATH once for all, and by GRACE through FAITH in him we are saved. But theologians are far from ideal, so we have a fancy word for the fancy study of SALVATION.

See also: atonement; Christ (Messiah); Jesus; theology

sovereignty \sah-vrihn-tee\ n.

The royal idea that we are not, in fact, our own kings and queens.

Perhaps the most vile poem in the entire English language is *Invictus* by William Ernest Henley, which ends, "I am the master of my fate: I am the captain of my soul." (Vomit here. Then continue reading.)

If that were true, we would all sail our soul-ships right into the rocks of despair, death, and destruction. And although Guns 'N' Roses may disagree, we have no appetite for those things.

As Christians we recognize Another as the captain of our souls and the master of our fates. Thanks be to God! There is one greater than

S

us who is able to conquer DEATH, forgive sins, give HOPE, and turn mourning into dancing. This idea is known as the sovereignty of God—the idea that God is in charge.

But the idea that God is in charge is strange, because God's in-chargeness is always balanced by God's faithfulness. God is powerful and holds ultimate authority, but at the core of God's sovereignty are GRACE, LOVE, and FAITHFUL-NESS—not absolute power. In fact, God's power comes through weakness, which we see most clearly on the cross. With that power, God works for the good of all people. God even shares God's power with human beings so that we can be agents of God's love and MISSION in this world.

See also: immanence of God; all the omni- entries; transcendence of God

spiritual gift \SPEER-ih-choo-al-GIHFT\ n.

Any of the gifts God gives to individuals for the good of the community, which people tend to guard jealously.

Here is one of the stupidest things that Christians have ever done—fight over whose spiritual gifts are better! Don't believe us? Read 1 Corinthians 12–13, where Paul writes to some Christians who were fighting over just that issue.

Some thought wisdom was the coolest gift. Others prophecy. Others preaching. Others speaking in tongues. Still others, gobbeldy gookeldy, blah blah blah, wing ding.

Paul says, "Fools! Every godly gift is necessary, and nobody has all the gifts! Everybody gets some gift from God, nobody gets them all. You need each other." Paul said that the three most important or "greater" spiritual gifts are faith, hope, and love. These three gifts are available to all people of faith.

Paul lists other spiritual gifts and fruits of the Spirit, which include apostleship, prophecy, teaching, deeds of power, gifts of healing, assistance, leadership, administration, love, joy, peace, patience, kindness, generosity, faithfulness, gentleness, and self-control. This is just a representative list. We are pretty sure that if Paul had kept going, he would have included sarcasm, bacon, and sleep.

See also: church; spirituality

spiritual practices \SPEER-ih-choo-al-PRAHK-ti-sihz\n. pl.

Use it or lose it—the things you actually do to live out your relationship with the living God.

S

A wise snark once mused, "Going to church doesn't make you a Christian any more than going to a garage makes you a car." Millions of enlightened folks chuckled and then promptly stopped going to church, presumably because they got the phrase turned around and didn't want to become a car. (And no, we're not going ask the ice-breaker question, "If you were a car . . . ")

Going to worship doesn't automatically make you a Christian, but being a Christian does involve going to worship, where you engage in many of the core spiritual practices of the Christian faith, such as praying, praising, hearing the Word of God, sharing God's peace, communing with God's body and blood, confessing your sins, and receiving forgiveness. Being a Christian also involves doing a lot of things you probably wouldn't otherwise do—such as praying at home, reading the Bible, loving and serving your neighbor, taking time for daily devotional reading, giving your money away, having hope for the future, bringing a pan of lasagna to your ailing neighbor, and forgiving your little sister. Those, and many other devotional actions, are called spiritual practices. And trust us, you need them.

Just like you practice banging the keys to become a piano player— and continue to tickle the ivories in order to stay a piano player—you have to practice faith to become a Christian, or rather to remain a Christian. Unless you use it, you lose it.

To put it another way, it's about the relationship. Spiritual practices are the ways you live out your relationship with the living God.

And we don't want to hear all your sassy works-righteousness talk. Look, we know: God creates faith in us. That's God's work, and a good thing, too, because if it were up to most of us, we'd kinda slouch our way through making our own faith. We're pretty lazy, and something good might be on Netflix. And that's exactly the point. God calls us to bust out of that sloth and do something with ourselves. That mystery of faith demands our pursuit, calling us to learn and live and do more. Because if you're not praying, reading, serving, giving, and going to worship, you're worse off than a car with no motor parked permanently in the garage.

See also: praise; prayer; sacrament; worship

spirituality \SPEER-ih-choo-AL-ih-tee\ n.

An interest or concern for "spiritual" matter, which is often motivated by a personal interest in material matters.

Here is a little advice. Never trust someone who says, "I am not religious, but I am very spiritual." Let us translate this nonsensical statement into plain English: "I am interested in matters of faith, but I am too lazy to actually figure out what I believe; I am interested in matters of the Spirit, but I lack the discipline to truly follow the Spirit's call." And yes, such a person will use a split infinitive because they are too lazy not to split infinitives.

Spiritual but not religious? This is the sort of twaddle that leads to confusing taking warm baths surround by scented candles with a spiritual challenge—such as loving your NEIGHBOR as much as yourself. Or to confusing journaling (to the sounds of Yanni torturing some musical instrument) about your adventures with the waste paper basket with the spiritual discipline of loving God with all your heart, soul, and mind.

Christian spirituality is not for cowards. Jesus calls us to pick up our crosses and follow him. He calls us to love our neighbors, including our enemies. He calls us to be willing to suffer—or at least to sacrifice some of our comfort—for the sake of the poor. He calls us

S

to care about what God cares about—that all people are fed, have access to JUSTICE, and know God's LOVE.

If this doesn't appeal to you, try burning some lavender tequila incense. See if that helps.

See also: disciple; love; prayer; spiritual practices; worship

stewardship \STOO-**wuhrd-shihp**\ n.

The spiritual condition of living as if the fleshly attachment to property weren't so fleshy; believing that everything you own actually belongs to God.

The freshly married bride moved in to her new husband's house and declared, "Everything that is yours is mine and everything that is mine . . . is mine." The next day, he objected, "Hey, you're wearing my favorite sweatshirt!"

"I told you, everything that is yours is mine."

Stewardship is sort of like that, except without the estrogen rush. In the Bible, a *steward* is someone who manages a property that is owned by another. (One famous biblical stewardship passage is the parable of the talents in Matthew

25:14–46.) This arrangement was common in the ancient world—sort of like being married is today.

In the bigger picture, according to the Bible, the whole universe belongs to God. "The earth is the Lord's, and all that is in it, the world, and all those who live in it" (Psalm 24:1). This is not an exaggeration or some parable—this is literally true. The earth belongs to God. After all, God made it. It is not ours to wreck or destroy; God has put us here to manage it because we aren't the owners.

In the smaller picture this means a Christian lives as if all private property is really a gift from God. Since it belongs to God, take good care of it, and feel free to share it with God and others. After all, it isn't really yours.

See also: creation

suffering \SUHF-uhr-eeng\ n.

That which inspires well-meaning but ultimately unhelpful platitudes from others—often because others really don't know what to say.

According to Buddhism's First Noble Truth, life is suffering. The Second Noble Truth is that on your deathbed, you will receive Total Consciousness. Wait. Scratch that. The Second Noble Truth is something about desire. Anyway, this is a book about Christian theology, so why are you letting us get distracted by concepts from other religions? Now, where were we? Oh, yeah. Life is suffering.

S

Seriously. When you look at most human lives at most times and places in human history, there has been and still is a lot of suffering—an inordinate amount of suffering. An insufferable volume of suffering. Physical suffering. Emotional suffering. Individual suffering. Collective suffering. "I looked and saw how much people were suffering on this earth and it sucks" (Ecclesiastes 4:1, mostly). Worse, suffering does not happen in equal measure—some people suffer well out of proportion to what other people suffer.

Worst of all, those who suffer—be it on account of a broken relationship, job loss, major injury, serious illness, death of a loved one, political forces, unjust social systems—often have to put up with people trying to rationalize or minimize their suffering. For example, "God needed another angel" or "They're in a better place now." Such platitudes, though well-intended, often just add insult to injury—to the point where irreverent, snarky comebacks are the best balm. For example:

- "The Lord has a plan." *Oh, yeah? Does it come with dental?*
- "When God closes a door, he opens a window." *How does that help someone in a wheelchair?*
- "Our heavenly Father doesn't give us more than we can handle." *Too late. He just did.*

The book of Job is often the go-to Bible book when it comes to questions about suffering and why God allows it. The book's title character, Job, suffers catastrophic tragedy and loss. His friends come offering platitudes. Job won't have it. And, in the end, God won't have it. In the final chapter, God wants to punish Job's friends for shoveling bad theology! So beware the platitudes!

The good news of Jesus Christ does not include the promise that life will be devoid of suffering. Nor does it promise that suffering will make sense. But it does offer a way to live with suffering—indeed, a way through suffering. "Come to me, all you who are weary and carry heavy burdens, and I will give you rest" (Matthew 11:28). And it offers an endgame, namely, a new life when "mourning and crying and pain will be no more" (Revelation 21:4).

So we've got that going for us. Which is nice.

See also: cross; incarnation; prayer; theodicy

S

thanksgiving \thānks-GIH-veeng\ n.

Any prayer or action that admits you didn't do it all yourself, and yes, you did need a little help along the way.

Humans say "Thanks, God" in many ways. Some are better than others. In ancient times people would sacrifice animals in gratitude to the gods for a favor received. How cool is that?! In the United States, many families feast on a turkey on the fourth Thursday of every November as football players on television point toward heaven after they score a touchdown. Some people get tattoos.

Giving thanks is not something that we should save for a single day on the calendar. Giving thanks is even more than our prayers before meals. Ideally, our entire lives are an offering of thanksgiving. "In everything, give thanks," it says there in 1 Thessalonians 5. Easier said than done, that's for sure.

Maybe it's a matter of perspective. When we realize that God is the ultimate source of all things and that we are ultimately dependent upon God for daily food and drink, homes, family, good government, peace, loyal friends, lovely neighbors, good weather, and so on, we realize, Dang! God's got a pretty big job there taking care of me, everyone else, and all that exists. Perhaps thanksgiving begins with simple gratitude that God is God (and we're not).

See also: creation; offering; worship

theodicy \thee-AH-dih-see\ n.

From the Latin *theo* + *dicey*, the dicey theological attempts to explain why the Creator of the universe doesn't live up to our expectations.

Why is there evil in the good creation? Why is there suffering? Why do good things happen to bad people? Why do faithful people get sick and die? Why do some people linger at the end of life? Why are some children born with handicapping conditions? Most of the "answers"—and we use that term loosely!—to these so-called "tough questions" of faith fall under the category of *theodicy*.

Some theologians who engage in theodicy try to find ways to protect God's integrity and reputation from questions that God doesn't mind if we ask. Many books have been written on this subject. (The most popular is Kushner's *When Bad Things Happen to Good People*.)

We won't try to summarize all of the theodicies, but the "answers" range from "God permits evil but doesn't do evil" to "God gave us free will, evil is our fault" to "When God closes a door, God opens a window" to "Everything happens for a reason" to "God is doing the best God can with an imperfect creation" to "Always look on the bright side of life" to "When life gives you lemons, make lemonade." All of these statements are popular versions of theodicy.

Trying to answer hard questions is not necessarily bad, but we should remember that God and God's reputation do not need protection from us. When God closes a door, don't go looking for a window—scream and kick and yell and pray and pound and plead with God to open the freakin' door. That's how doors work.

See also: absence of God; apologetics; evil; free will; all the omni-entries; silence of God; suffering

theology \thee-AH-luh-jee\ n.

Crazy talk.

Unfortunately, though it will assuredly be the most witty and entertaining exploration of the subject, this modest volume will not be the last theological book ever published. Crazy talkin' has a long and distinguished tradition, and as long as there are people crazy enough to join the conversation, it will continue. Armed with the vocabulary we're helping you amass, you're well on your way to becoming a crazy-talk-o-logian. Slap that on your resume, and let the offers roll in. (If you tip the paparazzi, they'll shoot you from your good side.)

Combining the Greek word *logos,* meaning "word," and *theos,* meaning "God," theology means "god talk." As a practice, theology is the effort to make sense and sentences of the various things we know about God based on what God has revealed in the Bible and what we know about people and the world. Theology is a human thing. (When God talks to us, it is called revelation; when we talk about God, it is called *theology.*) It combines human reason with divine revelation—often described as FAITH in search of understanding. Sound like a huge task? Well, duh: this is God we're talking about.

In eras past theology used to be *the* -ology—theology used to be called "the queen of the sciences," meaning it was the most important thing to study. Why? Spend a couple centuries in HELL, and you might figure that out. The Enlightenment taught us that human reason—and money!—is more important than faith, and now theology is just considered one thing among many you can study. We're not saying we agree with the Enlightenment—we're just sayin'.

Among Christians, theology is related to revelation in much the same way as a chicken is related to its egg. Theology starts somewhere—even if it's the simple assertion of the existence of God. For better or worse, the Christian theological launching pad is a bit more complex. Christian crazy talk begins with that big, messy, many-faceted

T

library we call the Bible. For our theological claims and assertions to be Christian, they must play by the Bible's rules and be consistent with the God who meets us in there.

Based as it is on the Bible's revelation of a living, free, and faithful God, crazy talk will always be a bit crazy. But there's crazy, and then there's *crazy*. Throughout the centuries of Christian history, theology has been judged to be good or bad based on a number of criteria. Good crazy talk, like good logic, will be consistent and non-contradictory. It will seek to be faithful to its source, reflective of the TRADITION, and relevant to its moment. Good theology serves faith. Bad theology may contain inconsistencies or internal contradictions, ignore or manipulate the biblical witness, or push a picture of God, Jesus, people, or the world that supports a limited social or political agenda or ideology.

We also think that good theology should be funny or at least amusing.

See also: the entire book

theophany \thee-AH-fuh-nee\ n.

When God actually literally shows up—and trust us, we're literally using *literally* correctly.

God cares not for likes, shares, or retweets. When God really wants to let us know what on earth is happening, God shows up on earth. We mean God actually shows up—appears corporeally, more or less—in physical manifestation. This is a *theophany*, a fancy term derived from the Greek words for "god" and "to appear."

In the Bible, theophanies take several forms. Moses saw God in a burning bush that didn't actually burn and also later saw God's back side (hey, we're not making this up). The Israelites saw pillars of cloud and fire leading them through the wilderness. God showed up for Elijah in a "still, small voice." Isaiah saw God on a high-and-lofty throne. Ezekiel saw God on a heavenly chariot—sort of an ancient precursor to the snowmobile (or ATV, for those living in more tropical climes). Sometimes God shows up to top-tier folks like royalty, priests, and prophets. But other times, God shows to shepherds, escaped criminals, and children—and once to a virgin girl. But the point of the theophany isn't how God shows up, but the message God brings. God typically appears in high-stakes situations and brings an urgent message to act, trust, or boldly follow. Sometimes theophanies are brief, but sometimes they can be long. Come to think of it, we can regard the entire life of Jesus—God in the flesh—as a sustained theophany lasting more than thirty years. God has spoken a Word of love to the world . . . his name is Jesus.

See also: Bible; revelation

theosis \thee-OH-suhs\ n.

The process by which one is unified with God—which sounds like it could hurt.

"You've got chocolate on my peanut butter!" "You've got peanut butter on my chocolate!" Perhaps you remember those old Reese's

Peanut Butter Cup ads. They advertised the union of two great tastes. Well, theosis is *not* like that. Theosis is crazy talk for what happens when you join together unholy sinners with a perfectly holy God.

Theosis is emphasized in the Orthodox churches. It follows a simple logic. If believers are one with Jesus, and Jesus is one with God, then believers are one with God. Or at least they are on their way to being in full union with God. Just as God became human in Jesus, theosis (or "deification") is about human beings becoming God. What's that you say? Isn't that the ultimate in social climbing? Isn't that the original sin? Isn't that what got Adam and Eve into trouble—wanting to be God?

Well, okay. Theosis isn't exactly about the ungodly becoming God. But it is about how we become holy *like* God—perfected human beings, without all that sin and death encrusting us. Theosis is about how holiness begins in us in this life before being perfected in the next. Pass the peanut butter cup!

See also: incarnation; immanence of God; Orthodox Church

time \tīm\ n.

That which is on your side. Until it isn't. Or until it runs out altogether. At which point it will help to have God on your side.

We'll bet you didn't know that the song "Time Is on My Side" was *not* originally written and performed by the Rolling Stones. (Look it up! And you thought you weren't learning anything.) We'll also bet you didn't know that the New Testament talks about two kinds of time: *kairos* and *chronos*.

Stuffy theologian-types like to point out that the Greek word *chronos* refers to calendar time (think *chronology*), while the Greek *kairos* refers to the idea that it's the right time for something to happen. It's kind of all Greek to us, especially since the difference doesn't always hold up. In the Bible, time marches on. But now and then it also pauses for something momentous. Two of our favorite moments: "When the fullness of time [*chronos*] had come, God sent his son, born of a woman" (Galatians 4:4) and "For while we were still weak, at the right time [*kairos*], Christ died for the ungodly."

See also: predestination; providence

tongues (speaking in) \SPEE-keeng-ihn-TUHNGZ\ v. + prep. + n.

An iftgay of the Olyhay Iritspay (see 1 Corinthians 12:7–10) that nobody can understand (see 1 Corinthians 14:2).

On the first Pentecost (see Acts 2), the Holy Spirit came on the believers. They started speaking in foreign languages that they had never studied, and they were understood by foreigners who couldn't speak their language. Since then, during worship services, some Christians have been known to start speaking ecstatically in sounds that others don't understand. This practice is known as "speaking in tongues." When all of this speaking in tongues was getting out of hand in the church in Corinth, the apostle Paul wrote that only "intelligible words" should be spoken in worship (see 1 Corinthians 14:9–11). If you have never spoken in tongues, don't worry—the Holy Spirit gives different gifts to different people. The most important gifts of the Spirit are FAITH, HOPE, and LOVE (see 1 Corinthians 13).

See also: Pentecost; spiritual gift; worship

tradition \truh-DIH-shuhn\ n.

That which stands as the bulwark against unbridled progress, undue change, or the replacement of worn-out carpet in the church sanctuary.

Most folks think that tradition is "the way we've always done it." And if that is tradition, you are probably hotly for it or coldly against it, but not lukewarm about it.

But that ain't it. At least not in the Bible or in matters of FAITH. Tradition is best understood as truth that is "handed on" or passed down

to future generations. Tradition in the best sense refers to things that are central and of "first importance" to the Christian faith (1 Corinthians 15:3). In other words, tradition isn't the little things we fight over, like music, liturgy, or what the sanctuary looks like (or hand-washing; see Matthew 15:2). Tradition is really about the good news—about keeping it straight and simple (1 Corinthians 11:2) and paying it forward. In that sense tradition is one of the most important sources to draw upon when thinking about God.

See also: adiaphora

transcendence of God \tran-SEHN-dihnts-uhv-GAHD\ n. + prep. + n.

The rope lowered into the pit you have fallen in; the power that lifts you out of yourself.

Ever realize that the trap you are in is yourself? Ever come to understand that the prison that keeps you from being free is not only of your own making but is you yourself? God's transcendence—the idea that God is above or beyond—holds just the good news you need to hear: God is so far greater than you and loves you so much that you can count on God to lift you out of yourself. "'For my thoughts are not your thoughts, neither are my ways your ways,' declares the Lord" (Isaiah 55:8).

See also: immanence of God

T

Trinity \TRIH-nih-dee\ n.

The Father, Son, and Holy Spirit—not to be confused with onions, celery, and green bell pepper—one God in three persons.

If not the mother of all Christian crazy-talking points, this one's at least in the top three. In theological circles the DOCTRINE of the Trinity is like the 1975 World Series or the 1957 Chevrolet Bel-Air Hardtop—a classic and the embodiment of truth. As with baseball's perfect moments or collectible automobiles, controversies arise, passions heat up, and devotees never tire of discussing the mystery of the Trinity.

But how do you sum up the Trinity, God's being three persons in one God? Legend has St. Patrick using a shamrock to demonstrate how three distinct leaves comprise a single plant. Others have borrowed the triune images of light, heat, and sun, or even ice, steam, and water. Our personal favorite is onions, celery, and green bell pepper—the Holy Trinity of Cajun cooking, without which soups and sauces risk unforgivably heretical blandness.

Trinitarian theology is descriptive crazy talk; it describes who God is in God's personal essence. Like most theological descriptions, neither the word *Trinity* itself nor the full doctrine of the Trinity occur in the Bible, but both the word and the doctrine seek to describe accurately the God who is revealed in the Bible. Theology is always playing a catch-up game—it tries to catch up to the reality of who God is. Doctrine doesn't make God triune; God *is* triune. Our language runs to catch up.

For the first Christians, who had learned from Jesus the Son how to follow God the Father and who had experienced the coming of the Holy Spirit at Pentecost, referring to God as Father, Son, and Holy Spirit came naturally. The New Testament is full of Trinitarian affirmations, such as:

- "The grace of the Lord Jesus Christ, the love of God, and the communion of the Holy Spirit be with you always" (2 Corinthians 13:13)
- "So [Jesus Christ] came and proclaimed peace to you who were far off and peace to those who were near; for through him both of us have access in one Spirit to the Father" (Ephesians 2:17–18)
- "Go therefore and make disciples of all nations, baptizing them in the name of the Father, and of the Son, and of the Holy Spirit" (Matthew 28:19)

After a little time passed, however, people started to want a clearer description of how Jesus "fit in" with the Father and the Spirit. Were the three the same or different? Were all three God? You see what's happening here: human beings playing catch up. Looks like a job for THEOLOGY.

Those catch-up–playing theologians worked to understand what the Scriptures as a whole say about God, including mind-blowing passages such as this bomb that Jesus dropped on his mates: "I and the Father are one" (John 10:30). Or this one: "Whoever has seen me has seen the Father" (John 14:9).

T

Eventually, it was agreed that God is Trinity: three persons in one God; three persons (Father, Son, Holy Spirit) in one Being (God).

See also: heresy; ontology; theology; transcendence of God

two kingdoms \too-KEENG-duhmz\ n.

The shocking idea that God's right hand knows what God's left hand is doing.

A concept describing the manner in which God rules over us humans differently in two different realms—the kingdom on the left (the law) and the kingdom on the right (gospel). Right up front, there's a problem: we don't generally like the idea of a kingdom, much less

two of them. Kingdoms are so passé, so old-world, so eighteenth century. Sure, in the West, there are a few kings and queens left here and there, but these function mainly as tabloid fodder; they are hardly the autocratic systems they were in the Middle Ages. Furthermore, "kingdom" smacks a bit of patriarchy, doesn't it? What about *queen*-doms? Elizabeth I and II, Cleopatra, Catherine the Great! What were they? Chopped liver? As if God were a man!

The truth is that—this side of the Declaration of Independence— we don't like the idea of being ruled over. The idea that God rules over us as a monarch rules over subjects—well, that's just plain undemocratic! We should be able to vote for the kind of God we want, shouldn't we? And if we can't vote for the kind of God we want, shouldn't we at least be able to vote for the kind of rules God uses to govern us?

Put simply, the two kingdoms describe how God rules over us in two different ways at the same time. God rules over both our physical and spiritual lives, but God uses different methods in the two areas.

Here's how it goes down. The kingdom on the left is about physical existence. Through the kingdom on the left, God provides governments and institutions (including CHURCH!) to keep law and order, compelling our sinful selves to behave and heapin' up trouble if we don't. The physical world belongs to God, who created it—and God still rules it. Note that this means that scientific investigation and book learnin' are part of God's rule too!

The kingdom on the right is about our spiritual existence. Through the kingdom on the right, God provides the good news of Jesus Christ, transforming us into saints who do good works spontaneously, willingly, and out of love for NEIGHBOR. Here God rules through the Word, sacraments, worship, and the announcement that sins are forgiven. We are free!

The central idea here is that God as Creator is the Big Cheese, the Head Honcho, the Queen Bee, the King Kamehameha! Consequently, God isn't just in charge of what happens in church but also what happens everywhere else: in schools, in homes, in governments, in commerce, in religion, in nature. God is God over the secular as well as the spiritual realm. So if you have ever wondered if God is left-handed or right-handed, now you know the answer: God's ambidextrous!

See also: gospel; happy exchange; law; simultaneously saint and sinner

T

vengeance \VEHN-jihntz\ n.

That which the Lord saith "is mine"—so why do you thinketh it's thine?

Payback's a bit challenging to talk about when it comes to crazy talkin' about God. The idea that God pays back wrongdoing is all over the Bible, and not just in the Old Testament. Even "meek and mild" Jesus gets his vengeance on when he speaks to the religious leaders of his day. "Woe to you!" he promises over and over. But the same Jesus also said, "Father forgive them for they know not what they do" about those same religious leaders as they mocked him and watched him be crucified. If ever there was a time for vengeance, it was on the cross.

We think that Jules said it best in *Pulp Fiction*: "And I will strike down upon thee with great vengeance and furious anger. . . . And you will know I am the Lord when I lay my vengeance upon you!" Actually, scratch that. Even Jules couldn't figure out what that meant. As we said, trying to understand the mechanics of divine retribution isn't easy. Take the Ten Commandments (please!): in Exodus 20:5–6, God's vengeance is described as being multiplied by two or three—followed by a description of God's grace being multiplied by one thousand!

In the end, we are left with the teaching of Rabbi Jesus who said in Matthew 5, "You have heard it said, 'An eye for an eye and a tooth for a tooth.' But I say to you, when someone smacks you upside the head, let them smack you upside the other head." Or something like that. Then he said something about "Loving your enemies." Then he may have added: "And you will know I am the Lord when I lay my restraint and forbearance upon you!"

See also: anger of God; grace; justice; Pulp Fiction; Ten Commandments; theodicy

vocation \voh-kĀ-shuhn\ n.

The heavenly idea that God cares about what you do all the time—not just when you are in church.

Got that? *Vocation*—not to be confused with *vacation* (taking a break from things) or *evacuation* (getting stuff out of your system)—is the thing(s) you are called by God to do with the gifts and talents God

has given you and to which you commit your passion and excitement and energy for the sake of God's CREATION.

The word comes from a Latin term, *vocare,* meaning "calling." This implies a caller: God. God calls more than just pastors. God calls each of us, gives us many gifts, and gives us a lift up by means of the Spirit. Actually, we all have more than one vocation. Our Christian vocations include our jobs and our roles as family members, friends, neighbors, citizens, and so on. Vocation is all about loving the NEIGHBOR and serving in God's name.

See also: bishop; laity; pastor/priest; spiritual gift

V

wisdom \WIHZ-**duhm**\ n.

(1) Knowing when to correct your mother, when to be your brother's keeper, and when to shut your trap; (2) the aspect of God's will that is built into creation itself, often personified in feminine form, because mother—whom you never correct—always knows best.

Remember that time when you got baited into a political debate on social media? Someone posted something amazingly stupid, and you just couldn't resist. You knew it was a bad idea, but, you know, you are you. So you couldn't just let it go.

Wisdom is a spiritual gift that most often comes with age. And most often, wisdom concerns itself with the bread-and-butter and meat-and-potatoes of the life of faith. It has less to do with the sort of super-fancy theological and philosophic reflections of professors and more to do with keeping your calm when your mother-in-law tries to start an argument on Christmas Eve.

What we're talking about here is God's wisdom. While we could describe this many ways, perhaps the most simple way would be to call it the way that leads to life in its fullest sense. God's wisdom creates a way through life that keeps you from being the clumsy, tongue-tangled doofus that you usually are. In pursuit of God's wisdom, believers not only get more smarterer as they age, but they also receive greater awareness, social skills, health, and peace. Do you remember that time when you had to keep listening to your roommate talk about backpacking through Europe and how she gained "just a way more open perspective on life"? Yeah, that's not wisdom. Wisdom was keeping you from rolling your eyes at your pretentious roommate, because you realized that—in God—there is always more to be learned.

And yes, you may throw that back at us when we start getting a little high and mighty on the multiple-degrees horse.

But back to wisdom, because God knows you need it. Wisdom can also refer to a particular set of books in Scripture—Proverbs, Job, Ecclesiastes, certain psalms (like Psalm 1 and 41), and also the books of Wisdom and Sirach if you're part of a Christian tradition that includes the Apocrypha. Proverbs is optimistic—follow the rules and life works better. Job is pessimistic—sometimes bad things happen to rule followers. Ecclesiastes is sort of a party pooper. Read it and weep. These books contain phrases and stories meant to teach about nature, life, humanity, and God. You know when your grandma starts waxing philosophical about life, and you wish you were writing it all down? Basically, someone did.

Speaking of your inexplicably wise grandma, wisdom has a third form as well, and she's a woman (see Proverbs 9). Scripture personifies wisdom as a female presence, sometimes called *Sophia* for the Greek word for wisdom (not just because it's a trendy name). Biblical literature personifies attributes often enough, so a personification of wisdom would not be unheard of. In Job 28, wisdom is described as a thing separate from God and known only by God. Then, in the book of Proverbs, Woman Wisdom speaks for herself and affirms that she existed before creation. Because of this, many have spent a lot of time on and given much effort to the pursuit of this figure. We find it satisfactory to know that Woman Wisdom finds a worthy place in Scripture and the understanding of God without trying to make the figure larger than it is. It's also nice to find a way to consider God that isn't so completely steeped in generations of testosterone.

May Wisdom guide you. And may it someday make you just as wise as your grandma.

See also: Bible; canon; creation; prayer

witness \WIHT-**nihs**\ n.

An earthen vessel that seeks to bear the heavenly to the unworthy in order to convince them of the improvable.

witness \WIHT-**nihs**\ v.

To talk about God to another person, which many people fear more than death.

Want to see your average Christian flinch? Ask them to share their faith. Publicly. (For readers who like a soundtrack with their theology, insert screaming sound here.)

To do so is to be a witness for Christ. Most Christians would rather be a witness against the mob than for Christ and would refuse to talk about their faith, even under subpoena.

Maybe we are reluctant to witness to Jesus because we think we are unable or unworthy to do it. "I can't do that! I wouldn't know what to say!" Sound familiar? But it's not rocket science or brain surgery or who wants to be a millionaire; it's really quite simple (maybe not *easy*, but uncomplicated).

Start here: everybody who believes has been witnessed to in some way, perhaps by a parent or grandparent, the care of a teacher, or maybe even by the earthen foolishness of a boring preacher. Think about who witnessed to you. Go and do likewise. Tell someone about Jesus in your own words, and do the right thing no matter what.

(Remember sometimes the things we don't say or do are a form of witness too!) That's the best place to start to witness.

And here's why it's so important: witnessing, or sharing what you know about Jesus and what he means for you, is how people are saved (1 Corinthians 1:21). Each witness tells Jesus's story through her own words. And God uses these words to bring people to FAITH. No fooling.

See also: disciple; evangelical; evangelism; martyr

Word of God \WUHRD-uhv-gahd\ n. or v.

A person, a book, and an event—all at the same time.

We dare you to ask ten people to finish this sentence: "The Word of God is. . . ." You'll get eleven answers. Or one answer: the Bible. But it's more complicated than that. The *Word of God* refers to (1) Jesus, God's Word to us (see John 1:1–4); (2) the Bible; and (3) any spoken WITNESS that the Holy Spirit uses to create FAITH and change hearts and lives. On top of that, the Bible says the Word is living and active (Hebrews 4:12) and unstoppable (2 Timothy 2:9), and it gets things done (Isaiah 55:11). So watch out: you might hear the Word of God, and then who knows what'll happen to you?

See also: Bible; Christ (Messiah); Jesus; sermon

works, good \gud wuhrks\ n.

What you do because you don't have to do anything.

Your friend invites you to dinner. You ask, "What can I bring?" Your friend answers, "Nothing, there is nothing you can bring, I've got it all covered." Out of gratitude, you bring something anyway.

Now, read this article again. But . . .

For "friend," substitute "Lord." For "invites you to dinner," substitute "saves you from your sins." For "bring," substitute "do."

See also: justification; sanctification

worship \WUHR-shihp\ v.

What God does to us when we think we're singing, praying, listening, daydreaming, and dozing on Sunday morning.

We know who you are. If you're a sports fan, you're sitting there at 11:50 on Sunday morning thinking, *If I leave right after Holy Communion, I can pick up the kids from the nursery, swing into the convenience store, and I'll still make it home for most of the game.* If you're married to a sports fan, you're thinking, *If you check the time once more, they'll call you Stump for the rest of your life.*"

Here's the thing about worship. We think we are the ones doing stuff. We sing, we pray, we kneel and stand, we give, we listen, we talk, we eat and drink, we sleep. But guess who is really doing stuff? God! When we gather weekly in worship, God speaks through the Word (which comes to us not just in the Scripture readings and sermon but in the hymns and the liturgy too). God speaks to us in the visible words of the sacraments. God forgives us through the words of the forgiveness of sins. God *happens to us* in worship.

And then God sends us out to join in God's MISSION to love, save, and bless the world. The Holy Spirit gathers us around Jesus Christ, speaks to us in the WORD OF GOD and the sacraments, and then sends us into the world to continue God's mission.

See also: means of grace; offering; praise; Sabbath; sacrament; sermon; thanksgiving

YHWH n.

Th Hbrw nm fr Gd, whch w dn't xctly knw hw t prnnc bcs th vwls wr lft t.

Make any sense of that? Okay, try this: *The Hebrew name for God, which we don't exactly know how to pronounce because the vowels were left out.* Hebrew—the main language of the Old Testament—was originally written without vowels, so we don't know exactly how the name YHWH was pronounced, although we're pretty sure it wasn't "Sean." (Come to think of it, we don't know how to pronounce Sean, either.)

Moses asked God, "Hey, what is your name?" God responded, "*'ehyeh 'asher 'eyeh,*" which some people think means "I AM WHO I AM." (Although like all things theological, this is also disputed.) In turn, some people think this is only sort of what the name YHWH means. And what *that* means is another question.

Out of respect for God, many pious devout Jews will not say the  name YHWH out loud—they either read "Adonay" (which means "lord") or "The Name" (which means, oh, you know). Out of respect for Jews, many conscientious Christians also do not say the name YHWH out loud.

Trivia: In most English Bibles, whenever YHWH appears in the Hebrew, the translation will say "Lᴏʀᴅ" (with small capital letters). But when the word *adonay* occurs, the translation will say "lord."

See also: God (or, as some Jews and others prefer, G-d)